Balance Exercises for Seniors

The Ultimate Fall Prevention Guide with Simple Home Workouts for Improving Stability, Mobility, and Posture

© Copyright 2023 - All rights reserved.

The content contained within this book may not be reproduced, duplicated, or transmitted without direct written permission from the author or the publisher.

Under no circumstances will any blame or legal responsibility be held against the publisher, or author, for any damages, reparation, or monetary loss due to the information contained within this book, either directly or indirectly.

Legal Notice:

This book is copyright protected. It is only for personal use. You cannot amend, distribute, sell, use, quote, or paraphrase any part, or the content within this book, without the consent of the author or publisher.

Disclaimer Notice:

Please note the information contained within this document is for educational and entertainment purposes only. All effort has been executed to present accurate, up-to-date, reliable, and complete information. No warranties of any kind are declared or implied. Readers acknowledge that the author is not engaging in the rendering of legal, financial, medical, or professional advice. The content within this book has been derived from various sources. Please consult a licensed professional before attempting any techniques outlined in this book.

By reading this document, the reader agrees that under no circumstances is the author responsible for any losses, direct or indirect, that are incurred as a result of the use of the information contained within this document, including, but not limited to, errors, omissions, or inaccuracies.

Free Bonuses from Scott Hamrick

Hi seniors!

My name is Scott Hamrick, and first off, I want to THANK YOU for reading my book.

Now you have a chance to join my exclusive "workout for seniors" email list so you can get the ebook below for free as well as the potential to get more ebooks for seniors for free! Simply click the link below to join.

P.S. Remember that it's 100% free to join the list.

Access your free bonuses here
https://livetolearn.lpages.co/balance-exercises-for-seniors-paperback/

Table of Contents

INTRODUCTION 1
CHAPTER 1 – WHY BALANCE IS IMPORTANT 2
CHAPTER 2 STRETCHING FOR BALANCE 12
CHAPTER 3 CORE IS KEY 29
CHAPTER 4 SEATED EXERCISES 43
CHAPTER 5 STANDING EXERCISES 70
CHAPTER 6 MIND OVER MATTER 87
CHAPTER 7: YOGA FOR BEGINNERS 92
CHAPTER 8 ADVANCED BALANCE EXERCISES 109
CHAPTER 9 IT TAKES TWO: TEAM EXERCISES 120
CHAPTER 10 DEALING WITH SETBACKS 132
HERE'S ANOTHER BOOK BY SCOTT HAMRICK THAT YOU MIGHT LIKE 137
FREE BONUSES FROM SCOTT HAMRICK 138

Introduction

Aging is part of the circle of life. The human body reaches its optimal state at age 30; then, it begins a slow decline. The decline causes individuals to start losing muscle mass, which leads to a loss of balance. Since seniors remain at higher risk for a host of illnesses and injuries, they must keep up with physical activity.

This book helps seniors regain their physical balance. Although this book focuses on seniors who are beginners, we have also included exercises for advanced-level seniors. Plus, all exercises have variations. You can perform an arm seated in a chair or standing.

We have sprinkled in simple tests that help you assess your current physical and balance level. For example, can you touch your toes? In addition, we remind you that walking, sleeping, and consulting with your primary care physician are all critical for a well-rounded exercise routine.

This book differs from others on the market because it considers the whole person. We looked at the things that impact seniors and the life that they might live. Plus, we outline several types of exercises and stretching.

Let's get started!

Chapter 1 – Why Balance Is Important

Aging gracefully begins with balance, and balance comes from healthy muscles. Healthy muscles have enough mass to protect the bones and joints. Plus, healthy muscle mass indicates that the individual has strength, an optimal range of motion, and agility. Moreover, healthy muscle mass suggests that the individual has taken steps to maintain it. Stagnant bodies lose muscle mass. Even those who exercise might lose some mass. Thus, it's a process to keep it.

Some seniors enter the late stage of their lives in decent health thanks to their genetic makeup. For the majority, it requires effort. Nonetheless, all seniors will deal with at least one health issue as they age, including maintaining a healthy balance. Staying in good shape in the later years means avoiding bad habits, participating in daily physical activity, having a solid bedtime routine, and having a healthy diet. Each element helps keep muscle mass at an optimal level. We'll explain why in this first chapter.

One day everyone will wake up and realize they cannot quickly jump out of bed. Instead, it takes effort. Sometimes the realities of aging set in as a rude wake-up call, and sometimes it's necessary. Finding out that balance is out of whack takes time. It's a slow process that can sneak up on seniors. It's as they say – it started slowly, and then it occurred rapidly.

Balance allows individuals to walk, stand, and sit stoically without giving it a second thought, like walking and talking; balancing becomes second nature. Once toddlers master the art of walking, sitting upright, and pulling themselves up off the floor, they stop thinking about the process. Instead, they just execute the action. As adults, people don't think about putting one foot in front of the other when walking. It's the same for balance – it just happens. In later years, pulling oneself off the ground from a sitting position is a different story. Once it becomes a challenge, it's time to take action. The inability to stand up from a sitting position on the floor without help indicates that balance is no longer at an optimal level. Thus, pay timely attention to the warning signs.

People rightly assume they will not tip over when standing, sitting down, or moving forward. That's why they don't pay attention to it when executing the actions daily. When a lack of balance becomes apparent, it's almost shocking. However, it's better to realize that the balance is out of whack before an injury occurs. It's never too late to regain balance. Depending on the timing, it's challenging or more manageable. Ideally, the realization encourages individuals to pay more attention to their lack of balance and take action. Those who pick up this book have taken a proactive stance for their health and balance – congratulations!

In technical terms, balance is a person's center of gravity. It is even weight distribution, so the left side is symmetrical to the right. Achieving equilibrium remains essential for balance. *Equilibrium* allows people to walk, sit, and stand upright without incident. Moreover, they will do it without overcompensating or favoring one side. If one limb or side works harder than the other, it will wear out the joints and muscles faster and lead to negative results. For example, walking in a new pair of shoes sometimes poses a challenge. The wearer must break them in and exercise caution with the first few steps, especially if the heels have some height. When the shoes cause discomfort, the wearer might favor one foot over the other. Favoring one foot or the other causes blisters, soreness, or calluses. It also leads to soreness on one leg – not ideal. When wearers distribute the weight evenly on both feet, neither experience more wear and tear than the other – that's great!

Understanding the importance of balance is vital for a person's safety. Furthermore, understanding the relationship between balance and muscle mass allows individuals to connect the dots. Most people find out that they will lose muscle mass as they age from a doctor, reading material, or the internet as it starts occurring. Others find out after it has noticeably progressed. They realize that something is off, so they search for answers.

Balance requires ongoing physical activity to maintain and improve it. It also requires a healthy diet. The nutrition and exercises that keep muscles strong benefit the rest of the body too. For example, muscles benefit from a nutritional intake of protein. Protein also improves oxygen flow in the blood and fuels energy. A diet and daily physical activity result in better balance and good health. We'll discuss several exercises that improve balance for seniors. Daily walking is a physical activity that keeps muscles fit. It's a low-impact cardio exercise that also benefits the heart, oxygen flow, and brain.

Staying away from vices such as smoking, consuming drugs, and drinking alcohol keep balance in good shape. Drugs and smoking prevent the muscles from regenerating themselves. Drinking alcohol to the point of inebriation is known to cause people to lose their balance. That's why the authorities have individuals perform a series of balancing tests. Instead of consuming alcohol, drugs, a bad diet, and smoking, spend your time eating well and participating in activities that positively affect the body, such as obtaining a good night's rest. For example, seniors benefit from sleeping seven to nine hours nightly. During sleep, the body recharges itself, and the muscles have an opportunity to regenerate themselves.

Scientists and researchers discovered long ago that the human body is a series of interconnected mechanisms. One depends on another.

The human body has almost 600 muscles that break down into three major groups – skeletal, smooth, and cardiac. Every skeletal muscle works with the body's nerves and brain to create movement. Thus, injury to the nerves or brain impacts the muscles too.

The aging process has a significant impact on balance. Other circumstances impact balance, too, such as accidents and injuries. It's a tough blow when preventing them isn't an option.

Those who experience equilibrium issues after a vehicle accident, workplace injury, or sports collision benefit from medical treatment right after the incident. In addition to medical care, many post-accident treatment plans will include physical rehabilitation therapy. Physical rehabilitation helps the muscles regain their strength. Plus, the body has a better chance of recovering full range of motion and agility during the healing process.

Accidents later in life have more negative ramifications since the body loses its ability to heal quickly and efficiently. Replenishing muscle mass becomes more challenging for the body with age. Nonetheless, it must remain a lifelong effort.

Medical studies show that the population experiences involuntary muscle mass loss after age 30! Given that the population averages a lifespan of 80 years old, individuals experience a decline of 50 years on average. Studies also show that losing between 3% to 8% of muscle per decade is normal. Mass loss isn't detrimental for a 30- or 40-year-old who exercises and eats a healthy diet. For those in their 50s and above, it's cause for concern, even if they exercise and consume healthy meals. **Remember that muscle mass loss negatively impacts balance.**

The involuntary loss of muscle mass occurs as the muscle fibers become thinner. It's similar to people losing their hair. The body simply cannot regenerate itself in the same manner anymore. It needs help through stretching, physical activity, and proper nutrition.

People experience several physical stages in a lifetime. The body reaches its optimal condition and then begins its decline. Toddlers learn how to walk as their legs become more muscular. Then, they learn to run, leap, and climb as their body grows and gains strength. Humans continue becoming more potent, agile, and flexible until their late 20s. At about age 30, the body reaches its peak and starts to wane down.

Remember that the decline is not obvious. Instead, how a person cared for their health in their 20s and 30s becomes evident in their 50s and 60s.

The good news is that it's never too late to improve your balance. Every day is an opportunity to engage in an activity that restores some of it.

Why having balance is hugely important, especially as a senior

Seniors experience several changes to their bodies and mental capacity. In addition to muscle mass loss, some will lose 40% of their hearing, and others will lose 40% of their vision. Age also catches up to the brain. An estimated 40% of seniors experience some degree of memory loss. However, the most common and dangerous peril that seniors face is injuries from falls. The loss of muscle mass combined with the loss of hearing, vision, and brain function lead to precarious results. Seniors can become disoriented more easily while trying to complete daily tasks. A slight distraction or hesitation becomes dangerous quickly. For example, if you decide to clean the kitchen cabinets, you might use a stepping stool to reach higher. Even though using a stepping stool to complete a simple task seems innocent, as a senior, it becomes dangerous.

Since balance comes from a healthy muscle mass, it indicates strength. People reach senior status at the age of 65. By this age, the body has declined for over 30 years. At age 65, people can officially retire and enjoy their later years. However, several health concerns exist too. Common diseases and chronic conditions in seniors include heart, cancer, respiratory, memory-related, and diabetes; by age 65, most ailments are apparent. The good news is that it's possible to manage several of them through daily physical activity and proper nutrition, and both help seniors maintain their balance.

An aging body becomes frail. A body that can't regenerate or replenish itself fails to recover from injuries. Moreover, it can't protect itself against them. Muscle mass protects the bones and joints against the impact of a fall.

Retirement age signals that it's time to enjoy life freely. To enjoy life to the fullest, entering it in good health is essential. Then, maintain it. It's less expensive to maintain good health than to pay for the ongoing medical care of chronic conditions. Therefore, if it's possible to prevent them or push them back a few years, it's worth trying. For example, the cost of this book is far less than the cost of hip replacement surgery.

In retirement, seniors' typical activities might include spending time with their extended families, gardening, social gatherings with friends, arts and crafts, and learning. However, some of these activities pose risks. Seniors have injured themselves while gardening. More commonly, seniors injure themselves when they fall while walking and completing daily activities.

Injuries to seniors are caused by falls

When seniors visit their primary care physician for an annual checkup, doctors judge the patient's ability to move freely. Limited range of motion, pain, and a lack of equilibrium signal that the patient needs to engage in more daily physical activity.

According to the Centers for Disease Control and Prevention, an estimated 25% of seniors fall annually. Every year, the senior population reports 36 million falls. Those falls result in 32,000 deaths annually. Moreover, three million seniors receive treatment in an emergency setting. Of the 36 million falls, 20% of seniors experience an injury. Common injuries include broken bones and head injuries. Keep in mind that older bones take longer to heal. The average bone break takes between six to 12 weeks to mend. For seniors, it takes more time.

About 300,000 senior patients require hip replacement surgery after fracturing one or both. Although patients can return home the same day after the surgery, it takes 10 to 12 weeks to return to daily routines. Full recovery takes between six to 12 months.

Senior hip injuries occur when they fall sideways. Falling forward results in knee, ankle, joint, and hand injuries. A backward fall is among the most dangerous since it can result in head injuries.

Interestingly, women fall more often than men – accounting for about 75% of hip fractures. Since women experience menopause, they undergo hormonal changes that impact their bones, body chemistry, and health. For example, osteoporosis affects women more than men due to menopause. The components of the human body continually regenerate themselves, including the bones, since they have living tissue inside them. Osteoporosis stops the regenerative process and causes the bones to become frail and brittle. Once the bones begin to deteriorate, falls become more dangerous.

Toddlers, teenagers, and young adults can handle falls. They bounce back up with a skinned knee, bruised shin, or scraped hand. Even though bone density hasn't reached its peak, toddlers can handle falls better than seniors. Why? The muscles and fat protect their bones and joints. For seniors, that's no longer the case.

There is also a financial aspect to avoiding falls.

Improved Balance prevents falls

Healthcare prices continue rising, even for those who purchase the best insurance coverage. A total hip replacement ranges between $31,000 to $45,000. Those who visit the emergency room after a fall can expect to pay $11,000 on average. To avoid paying expensive medical treatment bills, focus on prevention, such as strengthening the muscles and maintaining muscle mass.

Healthy muscles help prevent falls for seniors, as they will have the strength to keep the body upright and to protect the bones and joints in case a fall does occur. More importantly, healthy muscles lead to improved balance that prevents most falls, such as slips in the shower, standing on top of stepping stools, and tripping in the garden. Improved balance also provides agility that helps seniors catch themselves mid-fall, trip, or slip.

Health benefits of good balance

The health benefits of good balance are numerous. Since balance prevents falls, movement is more likely to remain pain-free and freer. Plus, there is less fear. Some seniors stop enjoying life fully since they fear pain and falls.

Good balance means fewer trips to the emergency room and fewer healthcare bills to pay. A senior's quality of life also increases. Retirement is the break people look forward to enjoying – retirement is the time to travel, try new foods, and learn more topics. These things are less likely to happen if seniors are not in optimal shape for their age.

As the average lifespan hovers around the 80s, it's at least 15 more years to travel, play with the grandkids, and take up hobbies. The health benefits of good balance also include pain reduction and ease of accessibility.

The opioid epidemic continues gripping the population. In the 1990s, the medical community noticed that prescription painkiller cases had increased. Painkillers became more potent thanks to opioids in the 1990s too. Painkillers serve a purpose. However, their newfound potency has severe side effects. Maintaining a solid center of gravity means seniors don't need prescription opioids to deal with the aftermath of falls. Instead, seniors can use homeopathic treatments for minor discomfort that comes with age. Healthy diets and physical activity help heal the body too.

Pain reduction

Once the body ages and its components begin to thin and wear down, pain starts to set in. Only 7% of individuals between the ages of 18 to 44 report experiencing symptoms of arthritis. It increases to almost 30% for people between the ages of 45 to 64. Once they hit 65, nearly 50% of seniors experience doctor-diagnosed arthritis.

Good balance results from healthy muscles that protect the bones and joints. Those who reach age 65 with stable balance will experience less pain. Since they don't fall regularly, they don't hurt themselves. In many cases, they also provide their bodies with proper nutrition and daily physical activity.

Pain that goes unchecked becomes chronic and impacts the brain. The brain records the causes of pain and its sensation. Before an individual reaches for a mug on a high shelf or takes several steps, the brain remembers that each activity causes pain. Moreover, the brain anticipates it. Therefore, individuals hesitate and might refrain from completing these tasks at all. Hesitation can easily lead to a sudden fall that causes preventable injuries. Even though a stepping stool is one foot off the ground, for a senior whose bones have aged, it equals a much higher elevation. Seniors with good balance have less fear and can confidently use their body's full range of motion. They can walk, reach, and stretch; the body requires stretching. Otherwise, the limbs start to become stiff. Stretching keeps the muscles limber. Therefore, it's possible to reach for mugs on top shelves.

So balance is essential for fall prevention; it's also crucial for keeping the muscles limber.

Even though a senior has entered their later years, the trick to maintaining good balance and a healthy body. Individuals who focus on prevention will experience less pain, falls, and injuries.

Ease of accessibility

Individuals in their 60s and beyond still have a lot of life to live. Those who have grandchildren and extended families will enjoy them more if they feel good physically. Seniors who opt to spend their retirement traveling or visiting with friends will enjoy the activities more if they maintain a good balance. Once pain or fear sets in, accessibility becomes challenging – mentally and physically.

Accessibility is controlling the body's movements and executing daily tasks. Seniors can fall on the way from their beds to the bathrooms – a common injury. They can also fall in the bathtub and shower – both are common causes of injuries. Falls occur on flat ground as much as they can on upward and downward slopes. Climbing the stairs at home also becomes challenging for those with shaky balance and stiff muscles. That's why some install motorized mobility tools along the staircases.

With good balance, seniors experience ease of accessibility. They can walk up the stairs in their homes without expensive aids. It's also possible to reach, stretch, and walk with ease. Playing with grandchildren becomes an enjoyable activity while exploring hiking trails remains an option.

The market share for devices that aid seniors in daily activities stood at $20.7 billion in 2020. Researchers believe that it will grow to $31.6 billion by 2028. The population will continue aging in more significant numbers, and the number of seniors needing aid devices will continue driving the market. Wheelchairs, walkers, and canes conveniently help seniors go from one place to another. However, the devices are cumbersome. Other devices that make up the senior aid market include toilet safety tools, medical beds, and scooters.

This book aims to help you achieve as much independence from medical devices as possible. Your quality of life can increase, and you'll spend less on medical care.

Reduced risk of injury

It's not possible to overstate the importance of balance. When individuals have a solid center of gravity, it improves their equilibrium. Even if they trip suddenly, their balance prevents them from completely falling, reducing the risk of injury. If you catch yourself with your hand, balance prevents significant injury to the wrist or ankle. Moreover, balance is a sign of good muscle and body health.

Everything in the body connects. If everything works in harmony, each component carries its weight. Thus, nothing works harder than necessary, so it remains in good condition longer.

Reducing the risk of injury improves a senior's quality of life. Living without fear, pain, and discomfort is a great way to enjoy the later years and retirement. It's also more cost-effective.

Eventually, age catches up to everyone. Therefore, engage in activities that allow the body to age gracefully.

Whether you have a good balance and want to maintain or improve it, the following exercises will help.

Chapter 2 Stretching for Balance

Now that this book has explored the importance of balance, Chapter 2 focuses on stretching for balance. Stretching establishes the foundation for improving and maintaining balance. This chapter will outline and walk readers through 8 stretches that help them warm up for the exercises that will enhance and sustain the balance described in the following chapters.

Several ways to warm up the body for exercise exist. For example, walking is an excellent warmup for jogging. Walking also remains the best physical activity that most seniors can complete daily. In a pinch, walk a lap around the block or house. Keep the pace steady and add the arms. With every step, move the arms back and forth. Adding the arms helps raise the heart rate and sparks metabolism.

Remember that walking is the best low-impact cardio exercise with several versatile features. Add it to your daily physical activity routine and the exercise routines we will outline for you in the following chapters.

Stretching is one of the key components of improving balance

Stretching is also versatile. It's one of the key components that helps seniors improve balance. First and foremost, stretching loosens the limbs, muscles, and joints. Some individuals might decide to exercise first thing in the morning. That's great! However, the body is at its tightest right after waking up. After a night of sound sleep, the body has rested, and the muscles have tightened. Completing some stretches right after waking up is a great way to loosen the muscles and prevent them from becoming so tight overnight. Therefore, if you wake up feeling stiff, start stretching daily. Stretching also helps lubricate the joints. Naturally lubricating the areas where the bones meet can help relieve discomfort during simple activities such as walking, reaching, and completing house chores. Stretching is the body's warm-up to handle the challenges of exercise.

In addition to sleep, age also causes the limbs, joints, and muscles to tighten. By the time an individual reaches the age of 70, the majority have lost 20% to 30% of their range of motion. Those who experience chronic pain, illnesses, and medical conditions lose a more extensive range of motion by age 70. Then, there is pain, a double-edged sword. Once a person starts to experience it, the brain registers it. When the body prepares to take a step, reach, or bend, the brain remembers how the pain feels and anticipates the discomfort. Therefore, individuals attempt to overcompensate by using different parts of the body to complete the task. Others restrict their range and hinder their flexibility and range of motion. Thus, begins the slippery slope. Stretching through morning tightness will loosen the muscles and limbs. It also lubricates the joints. The movement retrains the brain, and ideally, it will lead to less pain and discomfort.

Furthermore, the morning tightness will also subside. Once the range of motion diminishes, you might not regain it 100%. However, you can aim to recover enough to help you enjoy your later years.

The first step to improving and maintaining balance is to stretch daily. Suppose you do not stretch daily; at least stretch before starting any exercises we'll outline in this book. Therefore, start here and stretch.

Those who picked up this book have shown motivation to improve their balance. Good job! Now, assess your current state and previous experience. How often individuals participate in daily physical activity matters. Weekend warriors attempt to make up for their lack of physical activity during the week by going all in over the weekend – a risk for even the healthiest young adult.

Nonetheless, they're honest. Assessing how often you have exercised in the past sets you up for the future. Think back to the last time you exercised. It matters if the last time it took place was a month, year, or several years ago. It's essential to understand the starting point. Honesty makes it easier to establish milestones and goals. Since individuals who have entered their 60s and beyond lose flexibility, a balance between challenging the muscles and reality must occur. Stretching should challenge the muscles but not injure them. Therefore, consider running through a quick flexibility test.

Stand up straight with feet close together.

Bend the knees slightly.

Ensure that the knees and hips can support the weight.

Next, raise the arms all the way over the head.

Reach to the ceiling or sky with your fingertips.

Keep the arms next to the ears and stretch upward.

Assess how this feels throughout the body. If there is pain, take mental note of it. If this position causes a slight sweat or twinges of discomfort, take note of them too. Don't force the body to reach positions that cause it to strain. Reaching overhead is a light stretch; right now, it's only a test of flexibility.

If reaching toward the sky didn't bring on a lot of discomfort, move on to the next step.

Keep the arms overhead at the ears and start hinging forward from the waist. The goal is to touch the toes. Continue hinging from the waist with the arms at the ears and aim to touch the toes.

Assess if it's possible without forcing it. Remember that this is not a competition. The ability to touch the toes establishes the body's ability to bend and stretch. If touching the toes is impossible today, it might become possible in one month after completing the stretches and exercises outlined in this book. It might take six months or one year to accomplish the feat. The point is to try, consistently complete the activities, and continue trying. In the process, the limbs will loosen, the muscles will strengthen, and balance will improve.

Depending on the results of this little test, each reader will have a different starting point. All physical movement is beneficial once individuals reach their Golden Years. Some individuals enter retirement age with the ability to lift weights, run 5Ks, and participate in yoga and Pilates classes - either genetic inheritance or lifelong dedication to daily physical activity. Others will enter this age hovering around the average loss of flexibility.

This book considers that some seniors enter this period with limitations caused by injuries or illnesses that were not in their control.

This book will also address how to execute the stretches and exercises for those who experience chronic pain or illnesses or have not stretched and exercised for an extended period.

Just remember that the first step before completing any exercises is to stretch.

Before you start an exercise, read this chapter!

There will be days when you wake up and feel ready to conquer the day. Then, there will be days when the body does not cooperate. A flawlessly executed stretch or exercise yesterday does not occur today. That's normal. Expect to experience fluctuations in the body's abilities and work through them without forcing the movement. However, always stretch before completing any exercise outlined in this book. Although the seated practices from Chapter 4 seem innocent, warm up the body before starting anyway. The same goes for the standing exercises discussed in Chapter 5.

To emphasize the importance of stretching, this book will address the potential pitfalls of skipping stretching before exercising.

The body is like a rubber band composed of several fibers. Some new rubber bands require stretching before their first use, so they don't snap immediately. That's the same danger that individuals risk when they exercise without stretching first, *especially seniors*. They might not snap off a muscle, ligament, or joint, but you can pull a muscle that leads to a severe injury. In the professional sports world, hamstring injuries have become more common. These injuries seem to result from overuse of the hamstring and insufficient stretching. When injuries like these become common among professional athletes, *it's a warning for the rest of the public.* Learning from the injuries of professional athletes is beneficial for everyone else.

Stretching helps muscles *loosen and lengthen.* Exercising without stretching can cause them to shorten and become tighter. Tight and short muscles lead to the loss of flexibility and range of motion. More importantly, warming the muscles before physical activity prevents severe injuries, cramps, sprains, and spasms.

Stretch to loosen tight muscles and joints

The toe-touch test is a great way to gain insight into your current level of flexibility. It indicates the current tightness of the muscles and whether or not any pain and discomfort exist. Then, the stretches and exercises outlined in this book become more meaningful. You can create goals and take steps to reach them. Moreover, you can complete the stretches and exercises knowing your limits and reduce your risk of injury.

Let's start by looking at a range of stretches with instructions on completing them.

Range of different stretches

Several types of stretches exist; in general, the fitness and medical fields divide them into two categories:

- Dynamic
- Static

Then, the fitness industry and physical therapy professionals break dynamic and static stretching into additional subcategories, such as:

- Ballistic
- Passive
- Active
- Proprioceptive neuromuscular facilitation

In this book, the focus will remain simple. This book will outline dynamic and static stretches for seniors seeking to improve their balance. Plus, we will drop helpful tips throughout the book. Let's get started.

Static Stretches

When the fitness industry started, the professionals dispersed information and exercise plans based on the research that they had at the time. The industry used static stretches to help individuals loosen tight muscles.

Static stretching means entering a position and holding it for 30 to 60 seconds. The individual will feel the targeted muscle expand. Then, they switch to the opposite side and hold the position for another 30 to 60 seconds. Depending on the prescribed exercise regime, the instructor might ask the patient or individual to hold the stretch longer.

For example, a common static stretch is the standing hamstring stretch.

Start with both feet together.

Take a step with the left or the right foot.

Next, bend the knee of the back leg.

If you step forward with the right foot, bend the left knee.

Keep the right leg straight and the right foot flat on the ground.

Go deeper into the stretch by slightly hinging at the hip and keeping your back straight.

The hands can sit on the hips for additional balance.

Hold the position for 30 to 60 seconds.

This stretch lengthens the right hamstring muscle and along the leg. If the stretch causes discomfort, stay in the stretch for 30 seconds. Otherwise, hold it for 60 seconds.

Those who can handle the stretch can add another layer. For an added stretch, reach the right hand toward the right toe. This might add an extra layer of stretching. However, those who can still challenge themselves will touch the right toe and pull it upward. Hold this position for 30 to 60 seconds.

To complete this stretch, let go of the right toe and place the right foot flat on the ground. Unhinge at the hips and rise so that both the right and left legs reach a straight position.

Step back with the right foot so that it meets the left.

Now, take a step forward with the left foot and bend the right knee. Start hinging at the hips to increase the stretching sensation.

Depending on your flexibility, reach toward the left toe with the left hand.

If this is enough, hold the position for 30 to 60 seconds. Those who can go deeper into the stretch can touch the left toe and slightly pull up on it. After holding it for 30 to 60 seconds, let go of the left toe and start to return to an upright position. Straighten both legs and take a step back with the left foot so that it meets the right one.

Fitness industry professionals realized that static stretching is best after workout sessions. Holding a static stretch for 30 to 60 seconds prevents tightening after intense exercise. It can also help lessen the feeling of soreness the next day.

Dynamic Stretches

Dynamic stretches require the individual to hold the position for two to three seconds maximum. You should go into the stretching position and exits it for a set amount of time. For example, side lunges stretch the hips, thighs, and backside. Let's try it.

Start by standing upright with both feet slightly apart.

Now, take a side step with the right or left leg.

If you take a side step with the left, lean into the lunge by bending the left knee.

Keep the right leg straight.

Hold the bent knee and lunge for two to three seconds.

Then, return to the standing position. However, the legs sit in a V shape instead of side-by-side.

The position allows you to lunge again and hold it for two to three more seconds. In fitness classes, participants repeat the lunge on the same side eight times or for a set amount of time, such as in 45-second increments. When they complete the set on one side, they switch to the other.

From the V stance, bend the left knee and hold the position for two to three seconds.

Then, stand upright.

Next, bend the left knee seven more times or a set of 45 seconds.

Side lunges are versatile. Even though this book listed them as dynamic stretches, fitness trainers often use them as static stretches post-workout.

Dynamic stretches have become the type that fitness instructors and physical therapists use to help their patients warm up their bodies before exercise.

Full Body Stretch Routine for Seniors Seeking to Improve their Balance

1. Head Roll

Seated or standing dynamic stretch

From an upright position, roll the head in one direction fully and slowly. Then, the other direction.

Start by looking down and attempt to touch the chin to the cheek.

Then, roll the head to the left or right.

As the head rolls slowly, try to touch the ear to the shoulder.

Then, try to touch the back of the head to the top of the back.

Try to touch the ear to the other shoulder as the head continues rolling.

Then, return to the starting position to complete one rotation.

Complete eight rotations to the right and eight rotations to the left.

Take deep breaths and release them slowly during each roll.

Benefit: A stretch to help alleviate stiffness in the neck area. By loosening stiffness, you're less likely to injure the neck. If you wake up and feel stiffness in the neck area, try to relieve it with this stretch.

2. Neck Stretch

Seated or standing static stretch

From an upright position, stretch the neck in one direction fully. Then, the other direction.

Start by looking straightforward.

Extend the right arm upward.

Then, place the right hand on the top of the head.

Use the right hand to help lean the head toward the right ear and toward the right shoulder.

After reaching a comfortable position that stretches the neck on the left side, hold it for 15 to 30 seconds.

Take in several deep breaths and release them slowly while holding the position.

Then, release the hand and bring the head back to an upright position. Next, repeat the same steps on the left side.

Those who would like an extra stretch can repeat the sequence two to three more times. The stretch should lead to a feeling of relaxation.

Benefit: A focused stretch to help relieve stiffness in the neck area. By loosening stiffness and tension, you're less likely to injure yourself. If you wake up with stiffness in the neck, try to relieve it with this stretch.

3. Shoulder Roll

Seated or standing dynamic stretch

To continue loosening the upper body, shoulder rolls stretch the area. The stretch also helps release tension found stored in the upper body.

Stand in an upright position and keep both arms at the sides.

Point the fingers downward and avoid creating tension in them and throughout the arms.

Ensure that there is space between the neck and shoulders.

Now, lift the shoulders and roll them forward.

Roll the shoulders forward eight times.

Then, roll the shoulders backward eight times.

Benefit: Most exercises require you to keep your shoulders down instead of raising them toward your ears. This exercise helps you relieve tension in the area. It also enables you to feel the shoulders in several positions.

4. Rib Cage Stretch

Seated or standing dynamic stretch

Take a moment to feel the presence of the rib cage. Stretching the muscles surrounding the rib cage frees them up and improves breathing.

Stand in an upright position and place the hands on the hips.

Push the rib cage forward without pushing other body parts forward too.

The rib cage stretch is an isolation stretch. Thus, focus on pushing the rib cage forward only. Next, start rolling it to the right, twisting the hip, back, and opposite hip. Then return to the starting position, completing one rotation.

Repeat the rotation eight times to the right and eight times to the left.

Take a deep breath at the beginning of the rotation and release it slowly.

Benefit: Stretching the rib cage stretches the surrounding muscles too.

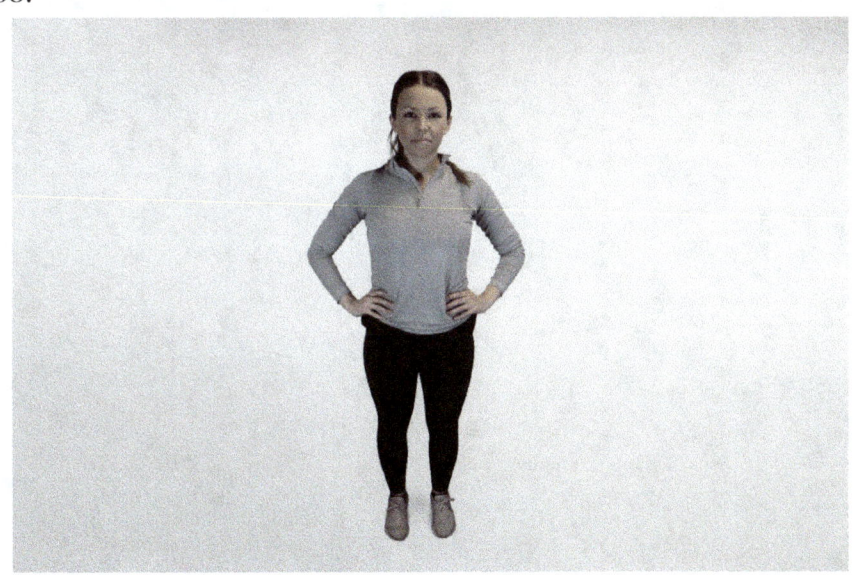

5. Hip Stretch

Standing dynamic stretch

The hip becomes tighter over time, even more for those who sit for extended intervals. Loosen them with this stretch.

From a standing position, place the feet hip-width apart.

Bend the knees slightly.

Shift the weight at the hips to the right in a swinging motion.

Then, shift the body's weight at the hips to the left.

Once you find your groove, shift the body's weight from right to left at an enjoyable pace. Shift the body's weight to the right eight times and eight times to the left.

Take a breath and release it with every other hip swing.

Benefit: Keeping the hips loose helps blood and oxygen circulation. Healthy hips also make walking, jogging, and running more enjoyable.

6. Hamstring Stretch

Seated or standing static stretch

To prevent hamstring injuries, warm them up before exercise.

From an upright position, take one step forward with the right foot.

Bend the left knee slightly until you reach a comfortable and challenging position.

Feel the stretch on the right hamstring and along the right leg.

Hold the position for 30 to 60 seconds.

If possible, lean into the stretch with the arm, hips, and back by hinging at the hips and stretching the arm forward.

Then, return to the beginning position.

Now, take a step forward with the left leg and bend the right knee.

You will feel the stretch on the left hamstring and along the left leg.

Benefit: The lower half holds the body's weight. Therefore, it's more prone to injuries than the upper half. Healthy and loose hamstrings make walking and standing easier.

Woman doing hamstring stretch

7. Calf Stretch

Seated or standing static stretch

The calf muscles perform essential functions during exercise, so keeping them loose is important.

Start with an upright position, and take a step forward with the right foot.

Bend the right knee forward so that the knee lines up with the toe.

Do not pass the toe with the knee.

The left leg remains straight with a slight bend at the knee.

For balance, place the hands on the hips.

You should feel the stretch *only in the calf area.*

Hold the position for 30 to 60 seconds.

Then, return to the starting position.

Take a step with the left foot and repeat the process.

Benefit: Tight calves are prone to soreness and injuries. By stretching, you prevent muscle tightness.

8. Ankle Stretch

Seated or standing dynamic stretch

Healthy ankles help prevent complete falls and sprains. Keeping them healthy starts with stretching.

Start with an upright position and lift the right foot off the ground.

Those who stand will have a chance to test their balance.

With the foot off the ground, make eight circles from the ankle to the right.

Then, to the left.

When complete, place the right foot on the ground and lift the left one.

Balance for a second or two.

Then, make eight circles from the ankle to the right eight times.

Then, eight circles to the left.

When complete, return to the starting position.

If you prefer to sit, find a sturdy chair that has no armrests.

Now, have a seat.

Scoot forward on the chair so that your back does not touch the backrest.

Place your hands around the sides of the chair for support.

Lift your right foot off the ground and keep the left foot planted on the floor.

Make eight circles from the ankle to the right eight times.

Then, make eight circles to the left.

When complete, return to the starting position.

Now, lift the left foot off the ground and keep the right foot planted on the floor.

Make eight circles from the ankle to the right.

Then, make eight circles to the left.

When complete, return to the starting position.

Benefit: Falls and trips commonly lead to ankle strains. To strengthen and keep the ankles healthy, remember to stretch them.

Stretching begins the journey toward better balance for seniors

The journey toward better balance begins with stretching. The stretching exercises outlined in this chapter will warm up the muscles, joints, and body for the exercises that follow in the next chapters. Some stretching exercises test balance. Therefore, it's a great way to test the body from the outset and set the tone for the following exercises. On off days, focus becomes more critical. On good days, consider challenging the body.

Let's explore core exercises.

Chapter 3 Core is Key

This chapter emphasizes the importance of building and maintaining a strong core on the way to achieving and maintaining better balance. Remember, seniors face several risks, and falls are the most significant risk. Everyone trips at some point. The difference is that some people will stumble and catch themselves; others will trip and fall. Individuals with healthy cores are less likely to fall all the way down. Trips that don't turn into falls are benign. If they start occurring more frequently and consistently, pay attention and take action. A strong core also strengthens the hips and lower back and leads to a strong trunk.

So this book will outline 7 core exercises, step-by-step. Then, this book will deliver three core-focused exercise routines.

Relationship between a strong core and balance

Seniors with healthy muscle mass experience fewer injuries, even if they fall. The muscles surround and protect the bones and absorb the impact. Nonetheless, falls remain dangerous for individuals over the age of 65. Therefore, it's wise to put effort into strengthening the core to help prevent falls.

A strong relationship between a healthy core and balance exists. Let's illustrate this point.

Seniors can complete most of the stretches from Chapter 2 in a sitting position. The sitting position affords individuals more stability. However, what happens if those stretches are attempted in a standing position instead?

For example, try the ankle stretch in a standing position instead of a sitting one. Even young adults have trouble remaining balanced during that stretch. The trouble with standing on one foot poses a challenge and a red flag. It signals that it's time to improve it and establishes a productive goal.

Let's start doing that.

What Is the Core?

You'll find the core between the diaphragm and the pelvic floor. It is situated in the abdominal muscles toward the back of the body, attached to the spine near the pelvis. The core also includes the oblique muscles. Together, these muscles help the body's trunk move. The core enables sitting down, sitting up, and remaining upright. It is the foundation that gives the arms and legs the force to move, and there are several ways to strengthen it.

On the outside, a flat stomach and defined abs indicate that an individual has a strong core. However, it's more challenging to achieve these visual effects with age. Therefore, judge the health of the core by the ability to remain upright, sit, and walk without discomfort.

This book considers that the health of some of its readers occurred from circumstances out of their control. For example, undergoing surgery impacts the body, as does having an accident such as a vehicle collision. Sometimes, the body doesn't recover to its previous state, and the incident leaves behind lifelong effects. Stretching and exercising help individuals regain some strength, muscle mass, and health. It can also deter the discomfort caused by severe injuries.

Importance of core muscles at an older age

A person's core muscles become more vital to overall health as they age. Since the body begins to lose muscle mass, strength, and vitality, individuals become more prone to injuries. The core acts as the body's center, the foundation for strength and balance. By strengthening the core, the rest of the body reaps the benefits too.

In Chapter 1, this book discusses how balance contributes to the individual's center of gravity. Now, this chapter will help explain how the center of gravity comes from the body's core.

Individuals with weak cores can expect to lose control over movements and eventually lose quality of life. If walking becomes scary, you are less likely to walk daily. Remember, walking remains an excellent low-impact cardio activity that delivers several benefits. If you shy away from it and don't strengthen your core, the act of walking becomes painful and dangerous. Moreover, Individuals with weak cores experience back pain, poor posture, and difficulty standing and sitting. In turn, these experiences cause additional adverse ripple effects. For example, back pain can become chronic and further decrease the individual's quality of life. Also, poor posture begins the cycle of joint discomfort.

We encourage you to test your flexibility and stamina at home through the simple stretches outlined in Chapter 2. You should also consult with your primary physician. To make progress, It's not necessary to overexert the body; it is essential to use it daily.

Inactivity is the fastest way to deteriorate the core.

Step-by-step core exercises

In the 1980s and 1990s, sit-ups and crunches became the best way to exercise the core. Then, things evolved in the 2000s; the physical therapy field grew, and the fitness industry continued its expansion. Moreover, these professionals incorporated science and data into their practices. They found different ways to strengthen the body, including the core. Push-ups, lunges, and sit-ups remain foundational exercises that strengthen the body, and this book will help readers work toward them. In the meantime, let's outline the modern core exercises for seniors. Are you ready to fly like Superman?

The goal of these exercises is to *help seniors help themselves.* We will explore seven core exercises from easiest to most difficult.

1. Superman Difficulty: Easy

For this core exercise, place a yoga mat or towel on the floor.

Lay on it stomach-down and look at the floor to keep the neck level with the spine.

Place the hands on either side of the shoulders with the palms down and flex the feet.

Then, point the toes and plant them on the ground.

Take a breath and lift the chest and hands slightly off the ground, keeping the hands level with the chest.

On the lift, avoid curving the spine and contracting the abdominal muscles.

Hold the position for 5 to 10 seconds and breathe out before returning to the starting position.

Target: The pose challenges the upper and lower back.

Benefit: The Superman move is a full-body floor balancing pose. You'll work your arms, shoulders, and backside.

2. Side Bends Difficulty: Easy

Start from a standing position with feet hip-width apart.

Place the arms on both sides tension-free.

Then, lift the right arm and stretch it to the ceiling.

Next, bend the elbow over the head, lean to the right with the arm, and take a breath.

Feel the stretch on the right oblique and contract the abdominal muscles.

Hold the position for 5 to 10 seconds.

Exhale, and then return to the starting position.

Repeat the same steps on the left side.

Target: Side bends engage the abs, hips, and thigh muscles. It's a simple exercise that lengthens your core and sides.

Benefit: Side bends strengthen and stretch the trunk muscles.

3. Dead Bugs Difficulty: Medium

Lay on a yoga mat or towel – on your back. Relax all the limbs.

Then, lift both arms and point the fingers toward the ceiling.

Next, bend both knees toward the chest and place them at a 90-degree angle from the floor. Avoid the temptation to bend the back.

Ensure that it touches the floor completely.

Take a breath and let the right arm fall next to the head while extending the left leg with a slightly bent knee and flexed foot.

Ideally, the stretched-out leg will hover slightly off the ground.

Bring the right arm back and left leg back to the starting position.

Then, let the left arm fall next to the head and stretch out the right leg. Let the right leg slightly hover off the ground.

Once you become comfortable with the coordination and switching of this pose, skip pausing as you switch the positions of the arms and legs.

Target: Core, spine, and back muscles.

Benefit: Since you'll lay on the floor and on your back, it's a supported way to work your core and back.

4. Leg Lifts Difficulty: Medium

Lay on a yoga mat or towel – on your back.

Ensure that your spine and shoulder blades continually touch the ground during the exercise. For extra comfort, place your hands under the lower back, palms down, or keep them at your sides. Straighten the legs, slightly bending the knees, and flexing the feet.

Then, lift the legs together slightly off the ground and hold them for a few seconds.

Next, lift the legs to a comfortable height and lower them to the starting position off the ground. Avoid over-bending the knees and over-lifting the legs.

Exhale on the leg lift, and breathe in on the way back down.

Target: Core, hamstrings, and backside.

Benefit: Since you're on the floor, you can safely work your core, hamstrings, and backside.

5. Bridge Difficulty: Medium

Lay down on a yoga mat or towel – on your back.

Place your hands at your side, palms down on the ground.

Bend your knees and start walking your feet toward your backside.

Keep your spine and shoulder blades on the ground.

The goal is to touch the back of your feet to your backside.

You also want to keep the feet close together.

Ideally, they will touch each other at the sides.

Exhale.

Now, lift the backside and lower back off the ground and pin the shoulder blades down.

Avoid putting too much pressure on any part of the body.

You should feel the burn on the backside and core.

Hold the position for 20 to 30 seconds before returning to the starting position.

In the bridge position, take a deep breath and slowly release it.

Target: Core, backside, and obliques.

Benefit: The bridge exercise is a safe way to strengthen your core, backside, and obliques.

6. Opposite Arm and Leg Raise Difficulty: Challenging

The opposite arm and leg raise challenge the core muscles. It also challenges the brain.

Start by placing the knees and palms on top of a yoga mat or towel.

Then, create a tabletop with your back.

Ensure that the shoulders line up with the hands and the hips line up with the knees.

Posture matters – it will avoid straining the rest of the body.

Stretch out the right arm forward and point the fingers.

Next, stretch out the left leg behind you while flexing and pointing the toes.

Hold this position for 10 seconds and return to the starting position.

Then, stretch the left arm forward and point the fingers while stretching out the right leg behind you and pointing the toes.

Exhale on the switch. Inhale while holding the position.

Target: Core, hamstrings, shoulders, and backside.

Benefit: Performing exercises that challenge the body and brain provides additional benefits. This exercise tests your balance, core, and coordination.

7. Planks Difficulty: Challenging

Planks are among the best core exercises for seniors, with several variations. We'll outline two. Let's start with forearm planks.

Start by standing upright on the back edge of a yoga mat or towel, facing forward.

Hinge at the hips and bend, attempting to touch your toes.

You can try to touch your toes, but it's not the focus of the exercise.

Instead, place your hands on the floor, even if you need to bend your knees.

Then, walk your hands forward.

As you walk your hands forward, straighten out your body and plant your toes on the ground. Once you straighten out your body, bend and plant the elbows and forearms on the floor. Place your hands palm-side down on the floor.

Then, keep the neck straight by looking directly down.

Now, contract the abs. Inhale and exhale at a steady pace in the pose.

Hold this position for 10 to 20 seconds to test your body.

To release the position, lower yourself to the floor.

To move back into the elbow plank position, move your arms under your body and lift the upper part with your elbows.

Then, plant your toes on the ground and lift the lower half off the ground.

Some individuals find the elbow plank more challenging than the full-arm plank. Both will work the core.

Let's take a look at the full-arm plank.

Start in an upright standing position.

Hinge at the hips and bend over until you touch the floor.

If necessary, bend the knees slightly.

Once you can touch the floor with your palms, walk them forward and stretch the body.

You'll reach the full arm plank position when you fully stretch your body.

Keep the arms close to the body, including the elbows, and line up the shoulders with the hands. Plant the toes on the ground.

Inhale and exhale at a steady pace in the pose.

Hold this position for 10 to 20 seconds to test the body.

To exit the full arm plank position, walk the hands back toward the feet.

When the hands reach the feet, roll the upper body back to a standing, upright position.

Target: Core and whole body.

Benefit: Planks work the entire body. They help individuals start gaining the upper body strength needed for push-ups. Like push-ups, planks work the core.

Now, we outline a core exercise routine using the exercises from Chapter 3 and stretches from Chapter 2.

Core routine

Medical professionals believe seniors benefit from a half hour of physical activity five days a week, or 150 minutes weekly. Each of the following routines delivers 15 to 20 minutes of continuous physical activity. Consider walking daily for 15 to 30 minutes to round out these exercises.

For each of the following three core routines, start with our complete stretch routine from Chapter 2 as follows:

Complete 8 head rolls to the right. Then, complete 8 head rolls to the left.

Hold the neck stretch to the right for 20 to 30 seconds. Then, hold the neck stretch to the left for 20 to 30 seconds.

Complete 8 shoulder rolls forward. Then, complete 8 shoulder rolls backward.

Complete 8 rib cage rolls to the right. Then, complete 8 rib cage rolls to the left.

Complete 8 alternating hip stretches

Hold the hamstring stretch on the right leg for 20 to 30 seconds. Then, hold the hamstring stretch on the left leg for 20 to 30 seconds.

Hold the calf stretch on the right leg for 20 to 30 seconds. Then, hold the calf stretch on the left leg for 20 to 30 seconds.

Complete 8 ankle rolls on the right ankle. Then, complete 8 ankle rolls on the left ankle.

Now that you've warmed up your body, let's exercise the core.

As you go through the exercises, mind your breathing. Remember to avoid straining other muscles.

#1 Easy Core

Side Bends

Complete 8 side bends with the right arm over your head.

Then, complete 8 side bends with the left arm over your head.

Hold each bend for 5 seconds. Then, release.

Superman

Start with 4 rounds of Superman, where you only lift the chest off the ground.

Those who want an additional challenge can lift the chest and lower body for the next 4 rounds. Otherwise, complete four more chest-only lifts.

Hold each lift for 5 seconds. Then, release.

Bridge

Complete 4 bridges. Hold the lift for 5 seconds. Then, release.

Repeat each exercise 2 - 3 more times.

#2 Medium Core

Superman

Start with 4 rounds of Superman by only lifting the chest off the ground.

Then, complete 4 more full-body lifts.

Hold each lift for 10 seconds. Then, release.

Dead Bugs

Complete 8 alternating rounds of Dead Bugs.

Leg Lifts

Complete 8 leg lifts.

Repeat each exercise 2 - 3 more times.

#3 Challenging Core

Bridge

Lift the body into the bridge position eight times. Hold each lift for 20 seconds.

Planks

Move into the forearm or full arm plank and hold the position for 20 seconds. Repeat 4 times.

Opposite Arm and Leg Raises

Complete 4 rounds of alternating arm and leg raises.

Repeat the exercises 2 - 3 more times.

After completing each routine, relax your body with the child's pose.

Child's Pose

Sit on your feet on the floor and tuck them under your backside bones.

Place your hands on your thighs.

Take a breath in and begin to roll your back over your thighs.

Keep your backside bones on top of your feet as you continue rolling forward.

If you feel that your backside bones start to lift, stop rolling forward.

Relax in the stretch.

Add to the stretch by stretching your arms forward.

For those who can sink deeper into the stretch, continue rolling forward, attempting to touch your nose to the floor.

Move your arms to your side, palms facing toward the ceiling.

Rest them on the floor and stretch them to the back of the room.

Relax in this stretch for several seconds – 30 to 45 will do. Allow your muscles, joints, and limbs to relax fully.

Importance of Persistence

The beauty of the exercises and routines outlined in this book is that they strengthen the core and balance with persistence. Even professional athletes must maintain their agility, flexibility, and strength. During the offseason, they can take time off to enjoy themselves. When they return to their routines, their bodies will feel the exercises for the first few days. That's why they attend training camps before their seasons begin again.

The first time you perform any of these exercises, you might feel challenged – that's OK! You might also feel soreness 24 hours after performing these stretches and moves – that's normal. The soreness will subside, and the body will persistently lubricate itself, especially the joints.

Importance of Routine

Routine exercise lessens the amount of soreness felt post-exercise. Plus, routines keep the body lubricated. Proper joint lubrication leads to less cracking and popping during daily movement. Routine will lead to looser muscles and a better quality of life.

Chapter 4 Seated Exercises

In Chapter 3, we focused on standing and floor core exercises. However, most exercises have alternatives. For example, seniors can perform side bends and leg lifts while seated instead of standing or on the floor.

In this chapter, we'll focus on seated exercises for seniors. Seated exercises help those with range of motion limitations. You can still exercise, maintain core strength, and improve balance since seated exercises contribute to healthy muscles, flexibility, and better balance. Then, you can work toward the standing versions.

If you fall into the advanced category, don't skip this chapter. We'll also outline some seated exercises that challenge you; just add weights.

The exercises in this chapter also benefit seniors who have experienced injuries or recently underwent surgical procedures. Both situations require rehabilitation. The sooner seniors work on their muscles, the more range of motion, strength, and flexibility they can recover. Seniors, in both cases, experience a few Catch-22s regarding exercising to improve balance. Some seniors skip participating in physical activity since it causes them significant discomfort. However, this leads to more pain in the long run. Remember that a body that doesn't receive physical activity loses its strength. The muscles lose their mass, and the body deteriorates faster and becomes more prone to injury. Plus, lack of exercise reduces balance. Essentially, it's important to take preventive steps, even in the golden years. Otherwise, seniors can develop chronic pain.

Age remains a significant factor for chronic pain. Between 50% to 60% of older adults report experiencing it. Chronic pain includes:

- Joint discomfort
- Nerve issues
- Back discomfort
- Headaches

It's tough to touch your toes if bending over ails your back. It's also difficult to focus on exercising if the aches in your head don't dissipate.

Chronic pain also limits flexibility and range of motion. Plus, it lowers the quality of life. In the process, the situation becomes a vicious cycle. Seniors who experience pain when they exercise will avoid it. However, avoiding physical activity worsens the pain. Again, stagnant muscles and bodies lose strength, flexibility, and range of motion. The physical therapy field has built its foundation on helping patients get past the pain. No one needs to push through the discomfort on the first try, but an effort to make progress has several benefits.

A great way to test your body's physical abilities is to start with the stretches outlined in Chapter 2. Remember to ease into them and avoid pushing the body too hard on the first few tries. If you can't touch your toes from a standing position, that's OK. The test determines your starting point and helps you establish goals. After four weeks of stretching, try to touch your toes again. Developing the ability to reach at least a half inch further is worth celebrating.

The following seated exercises help seniors who experience pain improve their balance – seated physical activity is better than no physical activity. Those who need rehabilitation from injuries or surgery can help the healing process. Seniors who try the exercises in this book but experience discomfort while standing will also benefit from the seated versions.

Some fitness professionals encourage their clients to mix up their exercise routines. They believe that focusing on the legs one day and the arms the next delivers better results. Some fitness trainers aim to surprise the muscles. Thus, seniors who can handle standing exercises benefit from adding seated versions to their repertoires too. Seated exercises become more challenging by adding weights. It's not necessary to add 10-pound weights to each hand right off the bat. Start with 2-pound weights and scale up according to your abilities.

For the chair, there is no best one for seated exercises. Whatever chair you have at home will do. If you exercise at the local recreation center, gym, or senior center, pay attention to the chairs they provide.

At home, ensure that your chair is stable – you don't want it to have wobbly legs. Ideally, it will have a backrest for reference, not for leaning onto during exercise. For the optimal range of motion, pick a chair with no armrests.

Let's get started.

Seated Stretching

1. Seated Overhead Stretch

Find your favorite chair and have a seat.

Plant your feet on the floor and straighten your back.

The position should push your body into proper posture.

Then, relax the shoulders and straighten your neck.

Now, place your hands on your thighs, palms down.

Without slouching, ensure that your body is free of tension.

Avoid overstraining any muscles and allow a sense of calm and relaxation to wash over you.

In addition, avoid leaning into your chair's backrest.

Most stretches and seated exercises require you to scoot forward in your chair instead of leaning back.

The outlined position is your starting position for all seated stretching exercises.

Now, lift both arms over your head and clasp the hands.

For additional stretching, stretch the arms toward the ceiling one more inch.

In the stretch, remember to keep your shoulders down.

Hold the position for 10 to 20 seconds.

Then, return to the starting position.

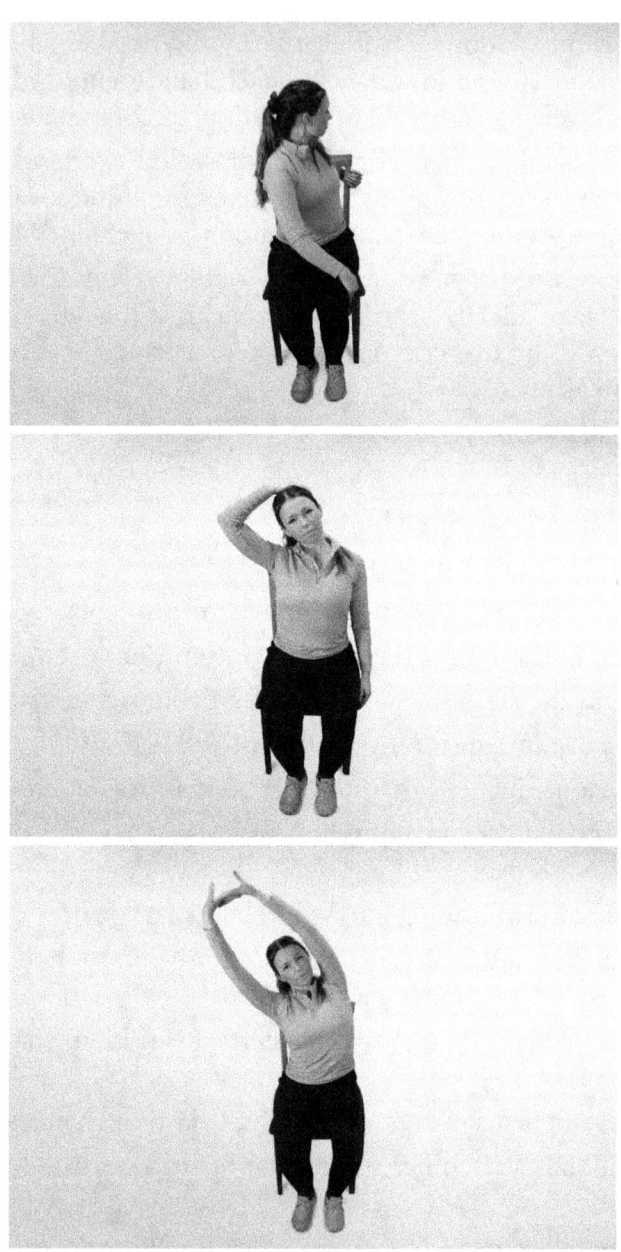

2. Seated Side Stretch

From the starting position, raise your right arm and slightly bend the elbow so that your right-hand hovers over your head.

Now, bend from the waist and lean into the stretch to the left. Hold this position for 10 to 20 seconds.

Then, return to the starting position.

Now, raise your right arm and slightly bend the elbow so your right-hand hovers over your head.

Next, bend from the waist and lean into the stretch to the left. Hold this position for 10 to 20 seconds.

Then, return to the starting position.

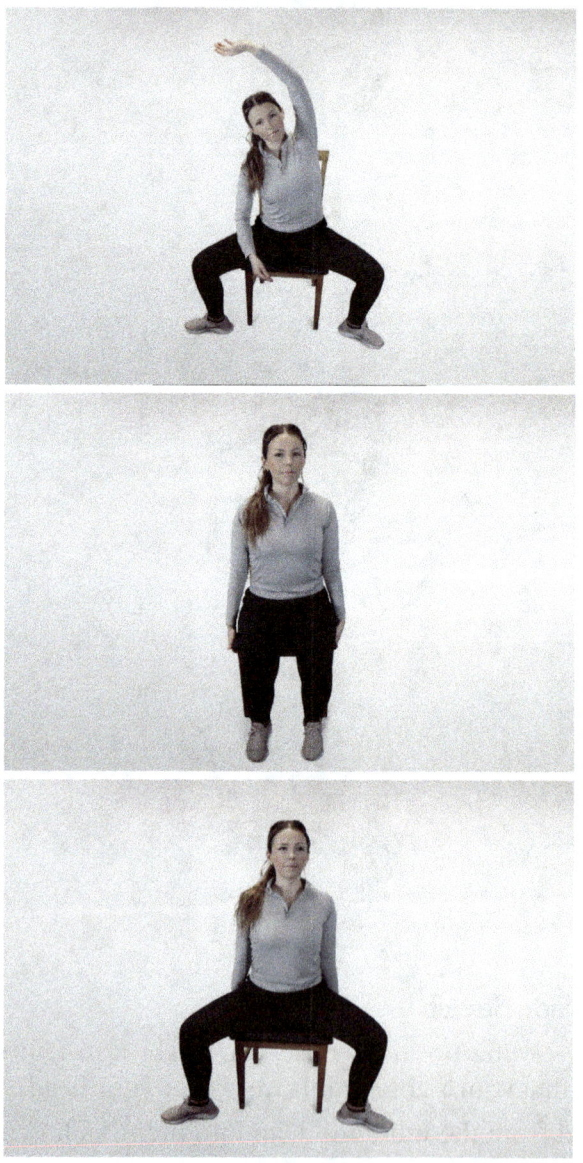

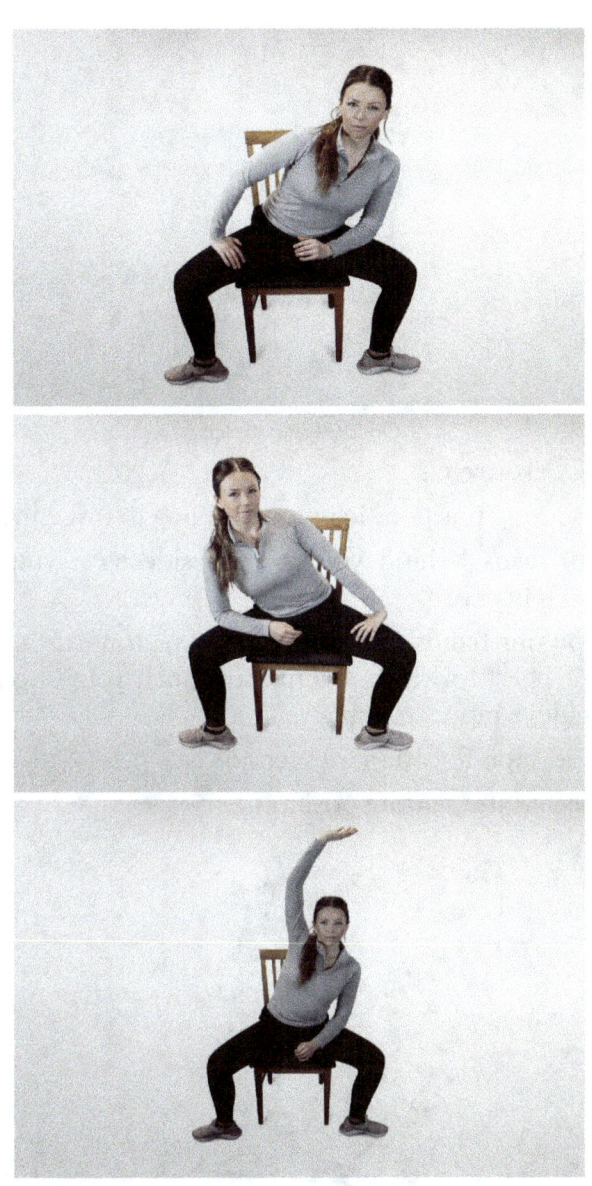

Goddess side stretch

3. Seated Chest stretch

From the starting position, lean forward two to three inches.

Reach your arms behind you at your side as if you're trying to touch the chair's backrest.

Next, clasp your hands and pull your arms toward the chair's seat and push your chest forward. Attempt to touch your shoulder blades together to achieve more stretch.

Hold this position for 10 to 20 seconds.

Then, return to the starting position.

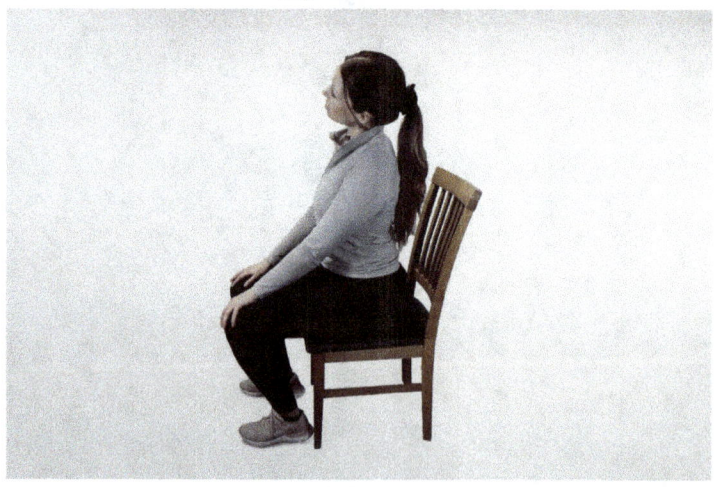
Chest stretch

4. Seated Arm Circles

From the starting position, lift your arms up at your sides as if attempting to take flight like a bird or airplane.

Hold them steady when the arms reach shoulder height.

Ensure that your shoulders remain down and not lifting toward your ears.

Stretch your fingers toward the walls. Now, simultaneously, make forward circles with your fingertips.

Allow the circles to become bigger and engage the entire arm.

Feel the stretch from the shoulders to the fingers.

Complete 8 forward circles and return to the starting position.

Lift your arms again at your sides.

When they reach shoulder height, start making backward circles with your fingertips.

Allow the circles to become bigger so you can engage the entire arm.

Complete 8 backward circles and return to the starting position.

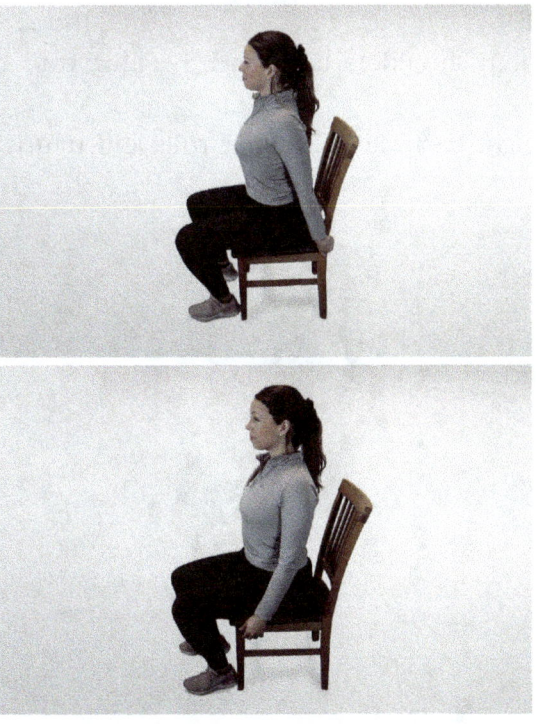

Arm circles

5. Seated Shoulder Rolls

From the starting position, double-check that your shoulders are relaxed.

Now, roll both shoulders forward, keeping your hands on your thighs.

Complete eight forward shoulder rolls and return to the starting position.

Next, roll both shoulders backward, keeping your hands on your things.

Complete eight backward shoulder rolls and return to the starting position.

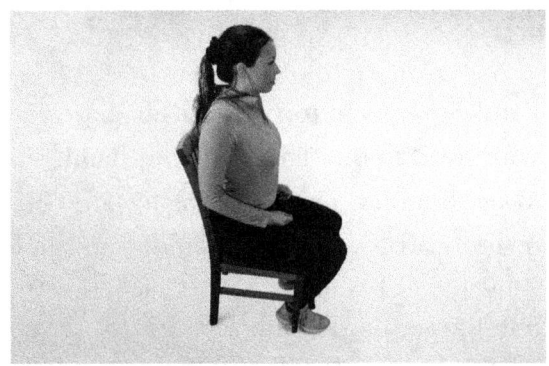
Shoulder rolls

6. Ankle rolls

From the starting position, lift the right foot off the floor about six inches.

If you need extra support, grasp the side edges of the chairs with your hands.

Next, roll your right ankle to the right eight times.

Then, roll the ankle to the left eight times.

When complete, return to the starting position.

Now, lift your left foot off the floor about six inches.

Those who need extra support can grasp the sides of their chairs.

Next, roll the left ankle to the right eight times.

Then, roll the ankle to the left eight times.

When complete, return to the starting position.

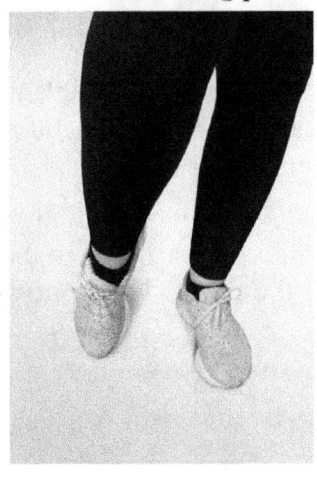

7. Neck stretch

From the starting position, lift the right arm and bend the elbow so that your right hand can rest on top of your head.

Gently pull your head to the right with your hand.

Ensure that your shoulders are not lifting toward your ear.

Instead, lean the head toward the shoulder and hold the position for 10 to 20 seconds.

Then, return to the starting position.

Next, lift the left arm and the elbow so that your left hand can rest on top of your head.

Gently pull your head to the left with your hand.

Lean your head toward the left shoulder and hold the position for 10 to 20 seconds.

Then, return to the starting position.

8. Spinal twist

From the starting position, check your posture one more time.

Ensure that your back is in an upright position and that your shoulders are not rising into your ears.

Now, grasp the right edge of the chair with your right hand.

Start twisting your spine toward the right and face your chest toward the right side of the room. Use your right hand to twist your spine more.

Hold the position for 10 to 20 seconds.

Then, release your spine and right hand and return to the starting position.

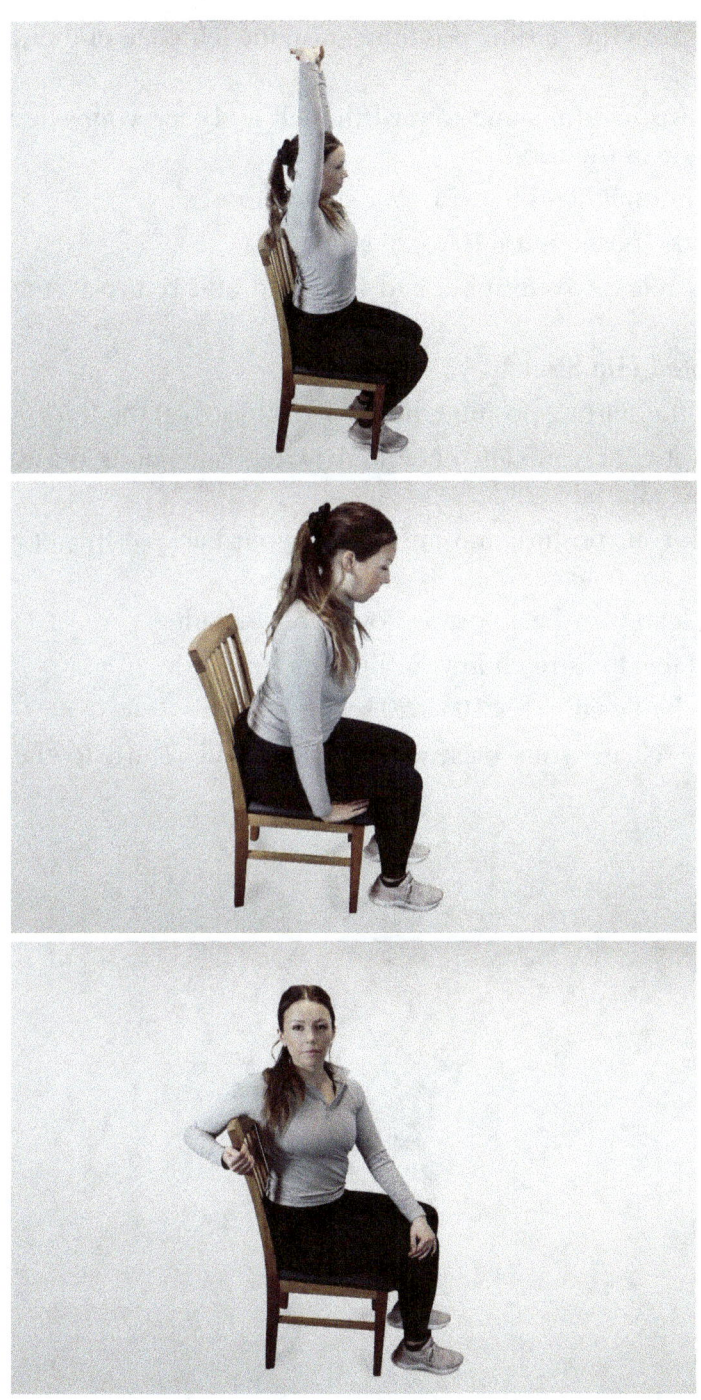

Now, from the starting position, grasp the left edge of the chair with your left hand.

Start twisting the spine toward the left and face your chest toward the left side of the room.

Use your left hand to twist your spine more.

Hold the position for 10 to 20 seconds.

Then, release your spine and left hand and return to the starting position.

9. Seated Hip Stretch

From the starting position, lift your right foot off the floor.

Cross it over your left knee and place your hands on top of the right knee and right ankle.

Check your posture and ensure that your back is straight and your shoulders are relaxed.

Now, lean your back forward over your right leg.

You'll feel the stretch in your hips and backside.

Hold the position for 10 to 20 seconds.

Then, release your back and right leg and return to the starting position.

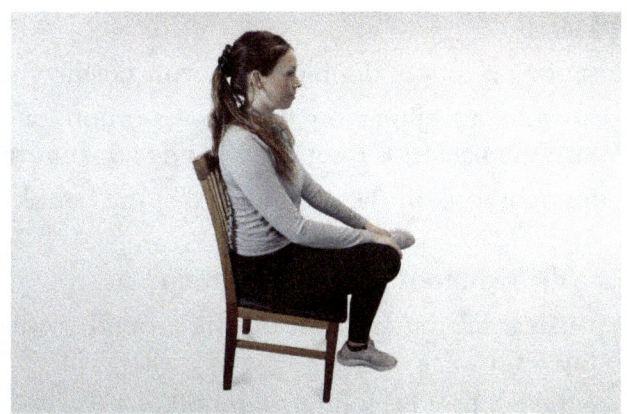

Next, lift the left foot off the floor.

Cross it over your right knee and place your hands on top of the left knee and left ankle.

Now, lean your back forward over your left leg.

You'll feel the stretch in your hips and backside.

Hold the position for 10 to 20 seconds.

Then, release your back and left leg and return to the starting position.

These stretches will warm up your body and prepare you for the following seated exercises.

Seated Exercises

From a seated position, you can stretch. It's also possible to perform some cardio and work the muscles. If walking isn't an option for you, the seated march exercise will help you achieve a similar cardio effect. Then, maybe you'll feel better and start walking again.

The benefits of walking remain well-documented. Some studies suggest that regular walking helps seniors expand their lives. Moreover, if you can walk for 30 minutes daily, it shows that you still have health on your side. Walking helps the heart pump blood throughout the body and helps the flow of oxygen.

Those who don't walk daily benefit from exploring why. If there is a fear of failing, it's great that you picked up this book. Ideally, you'll regain your confidence and experience fewer trips and falls.

For seated exercises, we'll use the same starting position as the seated stretches.

1. Seated March

From the starting position, double-check your posture.

Ensure that you are sitting on the front portion of your chair instead of toward the backrest. Keep your hands on your thighs.

Now, lift the right foot off the ground so that the right knee rises to hip level.

Then, place the right foot back on the ground.

Without pausing, lift the left foot off the ground so that the right knee rises to hip level.

Next, place the left foot back on the ground.

Keep your hands on your thighs to assess if you experienced any balance issues. If the exercise poses balance issues, try another round with your hands grasping the edges of the chair. Some will need to grasp the sides of the chair until their cores become stronger.

Continue marching until you feel comfortable with a consistent pace. You also want to become comfortable with marching in your chair.

Once you feel like you have obtained a consistent groove, add the arms. Adding the arms means letting go of the sides of the chair. Those who are not ready for this version of the seated march can move forward when they are ready – it's a significant milestone to set for yourself.

Adding the arms will cause your heart rate to rise. It's OK to raise it above your resting rate during exercise. Increasing the rate will cause more efficient oxygen and blood throughout the body. Plus, it allows your body to burn calories and pump your metabolism.

Let's start a seated march from the starting position again.

Lift the right foot off the ground so that the right knee rises to the hip level.

Then, place the right foot back on the ground.

Next, lift the left foot off the ground so that the left knee rises to hip level and place the left foot back on the ground.

For the next round, let's prepare the arms first.

Make fists with your hands and hold them at the sides of your hips.

Bend the elbows so that you make 90-degree angles with each arm.

In addition, make some tension so that you slightly flex your biceps.

Now, lift your right fist to eye level and push the left elbow toward the back of your chair.

Next, push your right elbow toward the back of your chair and lift your left fist toward eye level. Practice the movement a few times so that you become comfortable with the swinging motion. This movement alone will raise your heart rate.

When you couple it with your marching legs, you start reaping more benefits.

Let's put it together.

From the starting position, focus on positioning your arms first.

Make fists and form 90-degree angles by bending the elbows.

Now, lift the right foot off the ground and lift your left fist.

Then, switch without pausing.

Lift the left foot off the ground and your right fist.

In some ways, this is a total body move that works your balance and strength.

Continue alternating until you complete eight full sets.

2. Seated Knee Extensions

From the starting position, grasp the sides of your chair with each hand.

Avoid leaning back into the chair's backrest.

Instead, ensure that you remain sitting upright.

If necessary, scoot forward an inch or so in the chair, but keep plenty of your body on the seat so you don't lose your balance or feel you may fall.

Lift your right foot off the ground so that your knee reaches hip level.

Then, extend the right knee so that the leg becomes parallel to the floor.

Hold the position for 5 seconds.

Next, bend the knee and place the right foot back on the floor.

Now, lift your left foot off the ground so that your knee reaches hip level.

Then, extend the left knee so that the left leg becomes parallel with the floor.

Hold the position for 5 seconds.

Next, bend the knee and place the left foot back on the floor.

You can perform knee extensions in two ways – alternating or on the same side. If you opt for alternating, you will perform the exercise with the right leg and then the left – otherwise, complete 8 knee extensions on the right side. Then, complete 8 knee extensions on the left side.

3. Seated Calf Raises

From the starting position, grasp the side of the chair with both hands.

Then, sit on the front half of the chair instead of the back half.

Position your feet and legs hip-width apart.

Next, lift both heels off the ground but keep the toes and balls planted. Hold the position for 10 to 20 seconds.

Then, plant your feet back on the ground.

Complete 8 sets of seated calf raises.

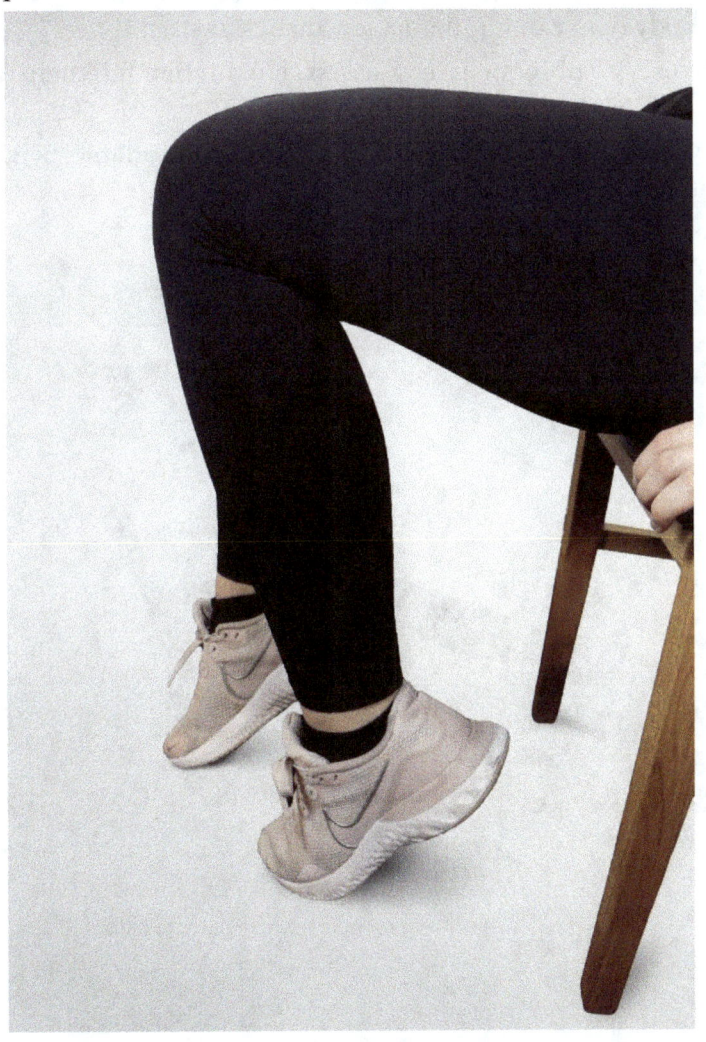

4. Seated Leg Lifts

From the starting position, grasp the side of the chair with both hands.

Then, sit on the middle portion of the chair.

Ensure that you feel secure and balanced in this position.

Bring your feet and legs together so that they touch.

Next, lift both feet off the ground simultaneously.

As you raise them and your legs, assess how your body feels.

If you can't lift the legs to hip level without overstraining other parts of your body, you can lift them a few inches to start.

With every subsequent try, assess if you can lift them an inch higher.

Every time you lift your legs and find a comfortable height, hold the position for 10 to 20 seconds.

Repeat the lifts eight times.

5. Seated Tummy Twists

From the starting position, make fists with your hands and bend your elbows.

Pin your elbows to your sides and place your fists palm-side up.

Sit on the front half of the chair.

Ensure that you have good posture for the best results.

Face forward and twist your tummy to the right.

Hold the position for 5 seconds.

Release the twist and face forward.

Then, twist your tummy to the left and hold the position for 5 seconds.

For an extra core workout, perform the exercise with an exercise ball.

The ball will stabilize your arms and help you concentrate your energy on your core.

In a pinch, making fists does create enough tension for the exercise.

6. Sit-and-Stands

Although Chapter 4 is focused on seated exercises, it helps to complete a seated exercise that enables you to measure your progress. Sit-and-stands help you assess how easily you can stand up from a seated position. The benefits of seated exercises for seniors remain numerous. They ensure that you can complete physical activity even though you need to rehabilitate from surgery or an injury. It's especially important for those who experience chronic pain.

Let's test your balance and strength with sit-and-stands.

From the starting position, scoot to the front half of the chair. We offer two versions.

Double-check that you have firmly planted your feet on the ground.

Place your hands palm side down on the chair, next to your thighs.

You will use your hands to push yourself off the chair.

Since you will push yourself up, ensure that the chair sits on a stable surface.

Slippery floors will not do in this situation! Also, avoid using chairs that have wheels.

Now, count to three and push yourself up to a standing position.

Assess how you did.

Try the exercise a few more times to gain a better assessment of your ability to perform the move.

Ideally, you will reach the point where you can stand up from the sitting position without pushing yourself with your hands – the second version.

From the starting position, scoot to the front half of the chair.

Double-check that you have firmly planted your feet on the ground.

Lift your arms parallel to your thighs and the ground.

Use your thighs and backside to lift yourself off the chair.

Count to three and stand up.

Assess how you did.

If this is too challenging, try using your hands a few more times. Plus, our other exercises will help you strengthen your torsi and lower half.

With Weights

Using weights with exercise provides several benefits. They create resistance and strengthen the muscles.

The following exercises are suitable for all fitness levels – simply alter the weight amount. For example, advanced seniors can add 10-pound dumbbells to each hand. Beginners or those who need to rehabilitate can skip the weights. Instead, create tension by making fists with your hands.

1. Seated Overhead Press

From the starting position, check that you have a good grip on the weights, one in each hand.

It's OK to test the weights a few times before completing the exercise. You want to challenge yourself without straining any part of your body.

Now, lift both arms as if you're about to take flight.

Then, bend the elbows and create 90-degree angles with your palms facing forward.

Next, take a breath. On the exhale, raise your arms straight up.

In this position, your elbows will sit next to your ears.

Then, lower your arms back to the 90-degree position.

Repeat the overhead press eight times.

2. Seated Triceps Extension

From the starting position, hold one weight in the right hand.

Raise the right arm as if you are about to complete an overhead press.

For support, place the left hand on the right elbow.

Then, bend the elbow and lower the weight behind your head carefully.

At the same pace, raise the weight back over your head.

Repeat the move eight times.

Next, switch the weight from your right to your left hand and lift it as if you are about to complete an overhead press.

For support, place the right hand on the left elbow.

Then, bend the left elbow and lower the weight behind your head carefully.

At the same pace, raise the weight back over your head.

Repeat the move eight times.

3. Seated Bicep Curls

From the starting position, ensure that you have one weight in each hand.

Position your elbows and pin them at the sides of your waist.

Create 90-degree angles with your arms and place your hands palms up.

Lift both weights toward your shoulders, keeping your elbows at your waist.

At the same pace, lower them back to the 90-degree angle.

Complete 8 bíceps curls.

4. Seated Front Shoulder Raises

From the starting position, place a weight in each hand.

Hold the weights like hammers, so your knuckles will face the floor.

Allow your arms to drop naturally to your sides.

If you need to scoot yourself to the foremost portion of the chair, do so.

Raise your arms so that the knuckles face the wall.

Bring your arms to shoulder level and hold them steady for two to three seconds.

Then, lower them back down.

Repeat the move a total of eight times.

Seated exercises benefit seniors of all skill levels.

As you read, adding weights makes them more challenging.

Plus, you can measure your progress.

Chapter 5 Standing Exercises

Standing exercises deliver the most physical benefits for seniors who want to improve their balance. When you attempt to stand on one leg and hold it, you'll find out quickly where your balancing abilities currently are. Floor and chair exercises round out solid physical activity routines, but standing workouts kick things up a notch. These exercises give seniors the confidence that they need to complete daily tasks.

For seniors, standing exercises pose the most challenges. Those who consistently engage in physical activity almost daily can work their way from seated exercises to standing ones. If the standing exercises in this chapter feel advanced, keep in mind that developing the ability to complete them is a nice goal to set for yourself.

Benefits of standing exercises

Completing some physical activity is preferred over performing no physical activity at all. This book included several seated exercises for seniors seeking to improve and maintain their balance.

To optimize your physical activity, performing the standing version is best. For example, you can also complete the stretching exercises from Chapter 2. You can even stretch your calves and ankles while seated.

This chapter will cover more advanced exercises; however, we will ease you into them. First, Chapter 5 outlines standing exercises that you can perform with the aid of a chair, serving as a balancing tool.

Once you gain your footing and sense of balance, we encourage you to perform them without the chair.

The benefits of standing exercises include:
- Better metabolism
- More calories burn
- Reduced possibility of weight gain
- Improves blood and oxygen flow
- Lowers cholesterol
- More muscle work
- Improves brain function
- Emulates daily movements

It takes more effort to complete an exercise standing up than sitting down. In the mid-2010s, researchers called sitting the new smoking. For a few years, they and some corporate consultants encouraged companies to help their office workers stand more often. Office furniture manufacturers developed standing-friendly desks and workspaces that some professionals adopted. The stations provided desktops with adjustable heights, and workers had the freedom to set their preferences. An office worker who stands during their shift can burn an additional 88 calories an hour! Sitting burns between 60 to 120 calories an hour, but standing can burn between 120 to 200 calories an hour.

As you complete the standing exercises, continually assess your body. Since this book focuses on helping you improve your balance, your goal is to improve at milestones you set for yourself. For example, how well will you do when you perform the standing balancing wand exercise?

Why standing exercises are effective

Standing exercises are practical for a few reasons. Standing requires all the muscles to work together. It's similar to walking – you engage your muscles when putting one foot in front of the other. Walking becomes second nature in the toddler years, so it's normal to forget that it takes a strong core, healthy legs, and excellent posture to execute the moves. Understandably, some seniors have trouble standing or walking for long periods. Whether it occurs through uncontrollable circumstances or age, continue participating in physical activity to improve your quality of life. Take small steps toward better balance and a stronger body.

The effectiveness of standing exercises also comes from the lack of obstructions. When you perform exercises on a chair, you bend your elbows and knees. The bends constrict the flow of blood and oxygen. Thus, you don't obtain the maximum benefits of exercise.

For the standing exercises, the starting position is standing up straight with arms and hands at your sides. Plant your feet on the floor hip-width apart and slightly bend your knees. Ensure that you have proper posture – your back is straight, and so is your neck. Double-check that there is no tension in your shoulders or neck. Relax your shoulders down instead of lifting them toward your ears. Stand next to your chair so that you can place your right on its backrest when needed.

You're ready!

Standing Exercises with a Chair

Reminder, for these stretches, the chair acts as a support tool. Even when you place your hand on it for support, it should be a light grip, not a heavy one. If someone attempted to remove the chair from under your hand, they could reasonably easily. Using the chair as a crutch when rehabilitating after an injury or surgery is OK. It's also OK to use the chair to gain confidence. However, the goal is to reach the point where you have the confidence and balance to exercise without it.

1. Calf Stretches

From the starting position, turn 90 degrees to face the back of the chair.

Lightly place both hands on the chair's backrest. Avoid leaning down to reach the backrest. If a chair doesn't work, you can always put one hand on a wall or countertop.

Ensure that your feet remain hip-width apart and that you have good posture.

Peel your heels off the floor and stand on your toes.

You'll feel the exercise in your calf muscles.

Hold the position for three seconds, then roll your foot back onto the floor.

Repeat the exercise eight times.

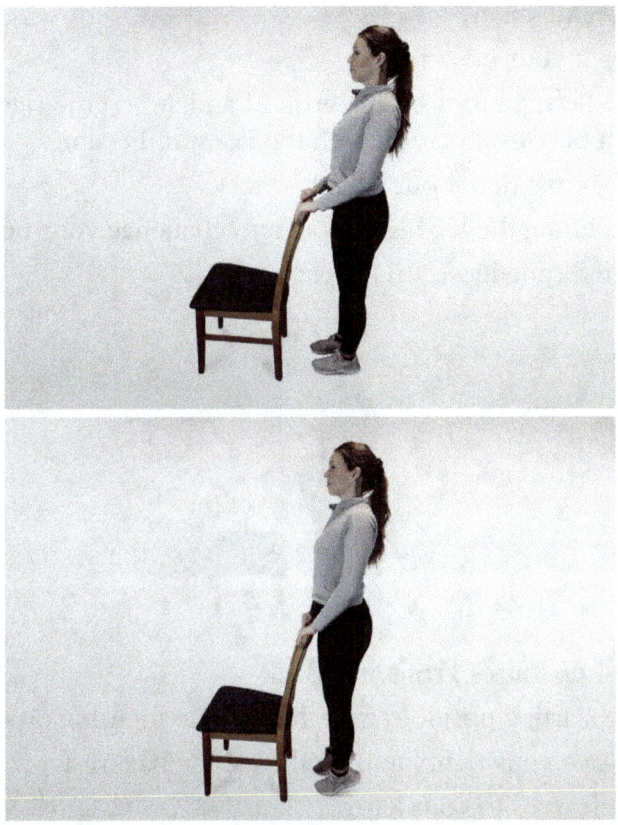

2. Side Leg Lift

From the starting position, place the right hand on the chair's backrest.

First, test your balance by lifting the left foot off the ground.

When you're ready, lift the foot off the ground and sweep the leg up so that it almost becomes parallel with the floor and ceiling.

In the first few tries, test the height too. Sweeping the leg higher doesn't always lead to a better workout. However, you want to challenge yourself. You'll feel the exercise in your backside and left thigh. With practice, you'll feel it in the saddlebag area too.

When you sweep the leg up, hold it at a comfortable height for one second and bring it back down. Repeat the move a total of eight times.

Then, turn 180 degrees so that you can place your left hand on the chair's backrest. Now, complete the exercise with the right leg.

From the starting position, check that you have lightly placed the right hand on the chair.

Also, check your posture.

Now, lift the right foot off the ground and sweep the right leg up so that it almost becomes parallel with the floor and ceiling.

Remember, it's not about height.

It's about lifting the leg high enough to challenge your body.

Complete 8 repetitions on the right leg.

4. Single Leg Raises Front and Back

From the starting position, we will continue focusing on the legs.

Lightly place your right hand on the chair's backrest.

Turn 90 degrees to your left.

Now, lift your right foot off the floor and sweep your leg up so that it's almost parallel with the floor and ceiling.

Point your toe.

Your goal is to challenge your leg muscles, not focus on the height.

You can challenge yourself by raising the leg, so it becomes parallel with the floor. You can also attempt to go higher. If you aim for height and lose balance, don't reach so high yet. One day you might raise your leg so that the shin or knee touches your nose like the Dallas Cowboy Cheerleaders – but *that day* is *not today* for most!

You'll feel the workout through the leg, including the backside, hips, and core.

Complete 8 repetitions with the right raising it forward.

From the same standing position, you can complete the exercise of the left leg.

Check your posture and hand.

Now, lift your left foot off the floor and sweep the left leg up so that it's almost parallel with the floor and ceiling.

Challenge the leg muscles.

If you find that you can lift your leg higher on one side over the other, that's normal. You can work to balance that out by stretching more on that side. You can also complete extra reps on the lower side.

Complete 8 repetitions on the left leg, raising it forward.

Now, you'll sweep the leg backward.

From the starting position, take one step back with your right foot and plant your toe on the ground.

Now, lift the right leg off the floor behind you.

You'll notice that your range of motion is far more limited than sweeping the leg forward or to the side. However, it's a great balance exercise that challenges the leg muscles and backside. The exercise motion becomes a pulse instead of a lift.

Complete 8 repetitions on the right leg, pulsing it backward.

From the starting position, take one step back with your left foot and plant your toe on the ground.

Now, lift the left leg off the floor behind you.

Lift the leg high enough to feel the burn on your leg muscles and backside.

Complete 8 repetitions on the left leg, pulsing it backward.

5. Mini Lunge

From the starting position, lightly place both hands on the chair's backrest.

Take one large step back with the right foot and slightly bend the right knee.

Now, bend the left knee but do not pass your left toe with the left knee; instead, *line them up.*

Hold the mini lunge position for 10 seconds.

To exit the mini lunge, straighten the left knee.

Then, step forward with the right foot.

Next, switch to the left side.

From the starting position, take one large step back with the left foot and slightly bend the right knee.

Now, bend the right knee but do not pass your right toe with the right knee; instead, *line them up.*

Hold the mini lunge position for 10 seconds.

Exit the mini lunge by straightening the right knee.

Then, step forward with the left foot.

The mini lunge is a versatile move. To perform it as a static stretch, hold the position for 10 to 20 seconds. To perform it as an exercise, you can complete 8 repetitions on each side or alternate legs and complete it eight times.

Therefore,

Step back into the mini lunge with the right leg, and hold the position for 10 seconds.

Step forward eight times.

Then, do the same on the left leg.

OR

Step back into the mini lunge with the right leg, and hold the position for 10 seconds

Step back with the left leg.

Hold the position for 10 seconds.

Step back to the starting position eight times.

Standing Exercises without a Chair

These standing exercises will challenge your balance and test your stamina. They will also indirectly work on your core and improve your balance.

The starting position for each exercise is a standing, upright position. Check your posture and relax your hands and arms at your sides. In addition, relax your shoulders and release any tension from the neck area. Then, position your feet hip-width apart.

1. Marching in Place

This book encourages seniors to complement these exercises with walking daily. For those days when you cannot go for a walk outside, you can march in place.

From the starting position, make fists with your hands.

Swing the right fist forward and the left fist slightly back.

Next, switch your fists.

Swing the left fist forward and the right fist slightly back.

Now, try the motions without pausing.

As you swing your fists forward and back, avoid twisting your waist.

You want the exercise to work your arms and raise your heart rate.

Next, lift your right foot off the ground.

The higher you lift your foot off the ground, the more challenging the exercise becomes. However, you also want to balance your current ability with height.

If you can lift your knee to hip level and continue marching, go ahead and do that. Some seniors can lift their knees to their chests.

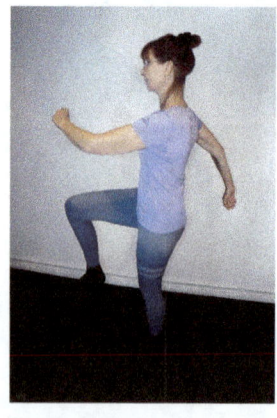

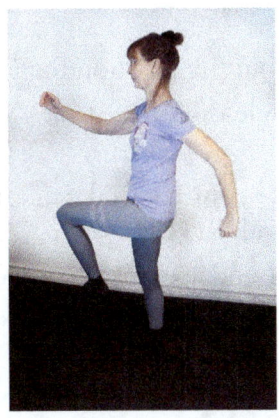

When marching in place, it's more beneficial to continue the movement at a steady pace regardless of foot height. A challenging, consistent pace will raise your heart rate, work your body, and help you burn some calories.

Therefore, march at your pace. Then, aim to lift your knees higher at regular intervals.

Complete 30 seconds of standing marching.

2. Lateral Toe Reaches (Alternating Side Lunge)

Now we'll incorporate exercises that make you stretch and reach. Keep in mind that it's OK to start small.

From the starting position, take a large step with your right foot to the right side. Your legs will form a V.

Next, lean to the right by bending your right knee and keeping the left one mostly straight.

With your right knee bent, try to touch your right toe with your left hand.

If you do not reach your right toe, that's OK. The attempt to touch it will stretch your legs, core, and obliques.

Hold the reaching position for 5 seconds.

Exit the lateral toe reach by releasing the reach and unbending your right knee. From here, you can switch to the left side.

Lean to the left by bending your left knee and keeping the right one mostly straight.

With your left knee bent, try to touch it with your right hand. It's OK if you cannot touch your toe; the goal is to reach a little further over time.

Feel the stretch and hold the position for 5 seconds.

Exit the position by releasing the stretch and unbending your left knee.

From the V position of your legs, take a large step inward with your left foot so that it meets with the right one.

You'll feel the stretch and exercise in several areas of your body, including your legs, obliques, and arms.

3. Lateral Step

The lateral step move is a dynamic stretch so check your starting position first. Ensure that you can securely plant your feet on the ground. It becomes a challenging standing exercise when you complete it eight times on each leg. Moreover, you can complete 8 lateral steps on one leg and then switch – OR you can alternate the right and left leg eight times.

From the starting position, take a large step to the right side with your right foot.

Plant the right foot and bend the right knee.

Line up your right knee with your toe.

Do not pass it.

Keep the left knee mostly straight.

Hold the position for 1 to 2 seconds.

Next, use the power from your right thigh, calf, and foot to push yourself back to the V position with your legs.

Now, bend the left knee and line it up with your left toe.

Do not pass it.

Keep the right knee mostly straight.

Hold the position for 1 to 2 seconds.

Next, use the power from your left thigh, calf, and foot to push yourself back to the V position with your legs.

Return to the starting position by taking a large step with your left foot inward so that it meets your right foot.

Complete 8 repetitions on each side OR complete 8 alternating repetitions.

4. Squat

The squat is a foundational exercise move that delivers several benefits. When squatting, it's important to check your posture. When you master the correct posture, then you can focus on going deeper into the move.

From the starting position, take a half step to the side with both your left and right feet.

Stand with your feet slightly more than hip-width apart.

Check your posture.

Ensure that your back is straight and that you have no tension in your shoulders or neck.

Clasp your hands together in front of you to create support. You can also stretch both arms in front of you, pointing your fingers. Keep the arms hip-width apart.

Next, bend both knees forward.

As they bend, sink into them a few inches.

As you sink, push your backside slightly to the back of the room.

Keep your back straight – do not arch your lower back. However, slightly push your chest forward.

Check that your shoulders remain relaxed, not lifting toward your ears.

In the squat position, assess how you feel. Hold the position for 10 seconds. Then, straighten your knees and bring your arms to the starting position.

Repeat the squat for a total of 8 repetitions.

Another option is to pulse in the squat position eight times.

A third option is to hold the squat position for 20 seconds. Then, repeat it eight times.

5. One-Foot Balance

From the starting position, you're going to test your balance.

Double-check that you have planted both feet on the ground.

Also, relax your arms and hands at your sides.

Release any tension that you might feel in your shoulders and neck area.

In addition, focus on something on the wall in front of you.

Focusing on an object will help your ability to balance on one foot.

You also want to start with good posture.

Now, slightly lift your right foot off the ground. This move is not a height test – it's a balance test. During the first few tries, it's OK to lift the foot off the ground a few inches only.

Assess how you feel during the one-foot balance.

Can you balance when the foot is only two or three inches off the ground?

Exit the balancing pose by planting the right foot back on the ground.

Next, lift the left foot off the ground a couple of inches.

Assess how you feel in the balancing pose?

Can you balance for more than 5 seconds?

Exit the pose by planting the left foot back on the ground.

6. Heel-to-Toe Walking

To further practice your balancing abilities, you'll try heel-to-toe walking next.

Heel-to-toe walking is the same test that authorities use when trying to find out if a driver is intoxicated or not. Even in a sober state, it's possible to lose your balance. That's why you practice, strengthen your muscles, and condition your body.

From the starting position, place your right foot in front of your left toe so that the left toe touches the right heel.

Next, place the left foot in front of your right foot so that the right toe touches the left heel.

Now, the space available in front of you determines how many more times you can repeat the exercise. Ideally, you'll step forward a total of eight times. If not, position yourself in your space so that you can. Then, start walking backward.

With your left heel touching your right toe, move your left foot behind the right. Ensure that your left toe touches the right heel.

Now, move your right foot so that the right toe touches the left heel.

Repeat for a total of steps or less if space is limited.

7. Balancing Wand

During the one-foot balancing pose, you kept your arms and hands at your sides. Now, you are going to move them up as if you are attempting to fly like an airplane. Extending the arms upward does make the exercise more challenging. Simultaneously, you can use your arms as balancing tools. If you lean to the left, tighten your arms, core, and trunk to prevent yourself from tipping over. The same goes for anyone who leans to the right. The strategy also works if you lean too far to any angle, forward or backward.

From the starting position, lift your arms up and keep them at shoulder height.

Lift your right foot off the floor two to three inches. Hold the position and assess your balance.

Ideally, you can hold the position for 10 seconds without tipping to any angle, side, forward, or backward.

Then, place the right foot flat on the ground.

Now, lift your left foot off the floor two to three inches.

Hold the position and assess your balance. Ideally, you can hold the position for 10 seconds without tipping to any angle, side, forward, or back.

Then, place the left foot back on the ground.

The balancing wand is a static exercise. Thus, work toward developing the ability to hold it on the right and left foot for at least 20 seconds.

Then, work up to 30 seconds.

Chapter 6 Mind Over Matter

At the beginning of this book, we pointed out that the brain registers pain and remembers it. Therefore, the thought of reaching or walking can trigger the sensation of pain before the body feels it. It's difficult to complete some tasks knowing that they will cause discomfort. Some seniors know that exercise will emphasize or reveal physical pain points, so they shy away from it. Many seniors know that working out will challenge their physical abilities, so they think twice about starting an exercise routine. This chapter addresses the apprehension and places a focus on mind over matter.

Seniors who have tried the stretches and exercises from Chapter 2 through Chapter 5 have tested their physical limits. Some seniors will discover that they are out of sorts physically. Others will perform each stretch and exercise without a hitch. For beginners, it's normal to find that balancing poses challenges or that completing 8 repetitions of any move requires effort. However, you have the motivation to see it through. After all, you've already read up to Chapter 6!

That's why you picked up this book - to improve your current physical ability. Moreover, you picked up this book so you can increase your quality of life and prevent injuries from falls.

Exercise and improving balance have two components; they require your physical self and also your mind. The most physically fit professional athlete can't compete to the fullest without confidence. Athletes must believe that they can throw complete passes, catch fly balls, and score goals. Otherwise, their performance suffers.

Therefore, a positive headspace during physical activity leads to better outcomes.

Seniors should exercise with a positive mindset. As mentioned earlier in the book, aging creates some physical Catch-22s. The body starts deteriorating at age 35. Once individuals feel pain in the knees, wrists, or neck, they start holding themselves back physically. For example, pushups become more challenging for those who have wrist issues. Knee discomfort will discourage others from walking daily. Knowing that most seniors have a physical ailment that bothers them, this book provides enough alternatives to put you on a path toward improving your balance.

Sometimes pushing oneself too far physically does lead to worse problems. However, physical rehabilitation is also a great way to lessen pain and prevent it from worsening.

If you have doubts about how far you can push yourself physically, consult with your primary care physician. Once they give you the green light, you can comfortably adjust your mental state. If your doctor advises you to perform our exercise routines as outlined, it's *go time*.

Let's discuss the mental aspect of exercising, the importance of having a positive mental attitude, and why exercise improves your mental health.

Mental aspect of exercise and balance

Seniors must take physical precautions that young adults do not. Young adults can trip and fall and come away with little to no consequences. For seniors, we have outlined that trips and falls have detrimental ramifications, including broken bones, injuries, and death. Moreover, seniors might have to exercise more slowly and carefully. Even though we outlined exercises with weights, you can replace them with lighter household items, such as canned fruit cans or bottles of water. It's all about judging your body and remaining honest about your physical limitations.

There is a difference between managing risk and not reaching your full potential. To improve balance, you must push through barriers, such as a lack of strength and limited flexibility. Previous injuries, medications, and fear are others. If you need to rehabilitate from a recent injury or surgery, we outlined sitting exercises that will help you regain your range of motion and strength. Then, you can move into the standing exercises.

Since every day is another opportunity to turn things around, it's OK to admit that you're a beginner. To improve, aim for the extra inch at regular intervals. Even if you do not realize the extra inch, trying keeps your muscles loose and joints lubricated. That's a good thing! Some physical activity is always better than no activity.

So what do you do when reaching for the extra inch causes too much discomfort? Remember that not trying to reach for the extra inch makes matters worse. Muscles that do not receive exercise will deteriorate faster. The loss of muscle leads to a weaker body that becomes more prone to falls and injuries – the opposite of what you're trying to accomplish by picking up this book.

If you feel discomfort, assess *why* you feel it. If you receive the OK from your physician, several things might cause your discomfort; not having stretched for over a year is one. Some people who don't stretch for a few days will feel stiff when they try again. However, the more consistently you stretch, the less stiffness you will feel if you skip a day or two.

Understand that the body does odd things. Today, you will go through all the exercises without any hiccups. Tomorrow, you'll also give 100%, but you won't achieve the same output – it's normal. Don't let frustration catch up to you. Keep a positive head on your shoulders.

When you exercise, your mental state impacts your performance every time. Therefore, bring a joyful, optimistic, and positive mental attitude. You're about to help your brain receive an extra dopamine hit, which will make you feel better. You're also about to help your brain release additional endorphins, which will brighten your day.

Benefits of a positive mental attitude

A positive mental attitude is a great way to overcome physical and mental hurdles. If you tell yourself that you can complete our series of seated exercises with 1-lb weights or our challenging core routine, you increase the probability that you will complete them – that's half the battle.

A positive mental attitude makes working out more enjoyable. Before the extra dopamine lands and the endorphins start floating around, you need to get yourself to that state. It takes warming up your body and raising your heart rate to achieve the physical and mental rewards of physical training.

In addition, a positive mental attitude lowers the possibility of injury during these activities. When you dive into improving your balance with joy, your focus sharpens. Focusing on the positive results of your sweat session helps you reap the rewards of your efforts. If you put your mind in a state to enjoy the workout, you'll work for the full 30 minutes. Thus, you'll reach your milestones and goals faster.

More importantly, a positive mindset keeps you motivated to continue improving your balance.

Motivation

Medical professionals believe that seniors should exercise 150 minutes weekly. You can break up 150 minutes into 30 sessions five times every week. Ideally, you'll participate in physical activity daily, such as walking for 30 minutes. When you add exercise to your physical activity routine, it changes things a bit.

After a workout, you might feel sore the next day. During the session, you may even feel some discomfort in some areas. Your body will also become stronger, and you'll improve your balance. It takes motivation to exercise almost daily; it takes additional motivation to improve physical areas that are tired or worn – or haven't been exercised before.

Thus, a positive attitude helps you consistently work out. Plus, the combination of exercising and a positive attitude improves your mental health.

How exercise improves mental health

The aging population faces adversity in several forms. We've discussed the physical ones at some length, but *mental health* is another. Some mental health conditions occur without warning and become lifelong ailments, such as dementia. The good news is that you can overcome a host of other mental health ailments like cognitive decline. Physical activity helps seniors prevent depression and anxiety disorders. If you work out with a friend or group of peers, you can also prevent feeling isolated.

The CDC points out that depression is not part of the *aging process.* While an estimated 19 million Americans experience some form of depression, organizations tend to pay more attention to seniors and signs of depression because this population is more prone to it. Seniors with at least one chronic illness experience more pain and discomfort. Thus, the condition can catch up to their mental state. As stated above, depression isn't because of the aging process, but the side effects of that process can lead to depression. The CDC points out that it's possible to address and overcome depression; it's treatable.

Working out leads to better mental health for a few reasons. First, it keeps your mind active. Like muscles, the brain also requires training to keep it strong and lucent. As you train your body, you also work your brain. Some individuals experience better moods, reduced stress, and increased energy levels after one workout session. If you consistently exercise, you'll notice that these benefits remain with you. Thus, you improve your balance and mental health.

Benefits of a positive headspace during exercise

A positive headspace during exercise prevents injuries and increases its benefits. Moreover, you'll achieve better results. You'll stay motivated and enjoy working out consistently.

Some ways to maintain a positive attitude in life are:

- Practicing gratitude
- Eating a healthy diet
- Having a sense of humor
- Focusing on the positive
- Avoiding negativity and negative individuals

To keep a positive attitude while exercising, try the following:

- Breathing properly
- Focusing on an overall goal
- Focusing on milestones
- Enjoying the natural high
- Remembering that you'll feel stronger

If you feel like you need additional help focusing, keep reading. We discuss how yoga benefits your mental health and how it helps you improve your balance.

Chapter 7: Yoga for Beginners

An estimated 33 million individuals practice yoga consistently in the United States. The benefits of the practice remain well-documented. More importantly, yoga is among the physical activities that children, adults, and seniors can practice. With a few modifications, yoga becomes challenging. Different modifications make it easy on the joints, muscles, and limbs. Thus, seniors can improve their balance and mental health by incorporating yoga into their physical activity routines.

This chapter will cover several yoga poses suitable for seniors, especially beginners.

First, let's discuss its benefits for seniors.

What is yoga?

The general consensus believes that yoga originated in Northern India almost 5,000 years ago. Over the years, yoga has evolved, but the practice has maintained its spiritual aspect. During the sessions, instructors will remind participants to connect the spirit to the body.

The practice has also broken off into sub-practices such as vinyasa, Bikram, and Hatha. Each sub-practice focuses on a specialty. For example, *vinyasa* is also known as flow yoga. Participants flow from one pose to the next without interruption. Participants also connect their breath with the movement; in Hatha yoga, the sub-practice places emphasis on breathing, then the controlled movements.

The westward yoga push started in the 1800s and carried over into the 1900s. The 1980s saw the practice catch on like wildfire. As mentioned earlier, yoga maintains a solid foothold among Americans decades later.

In short, yoga connects the mind and the body. Yogi practitioners aim to connect their spirits with their bodies. Nonetheless, instructors welcome students of all skill levels to their classes. Moreover, seniors can practice yoga from the comfort of their homes and at their pace.

How to get started

To start your yoga practice, check in with your primary care physician first. You want to obtain the green light from your doctor, who can provide some suggestions. Your doctor might recommend focusing on standing poses that help improve your balance, such as the tree pose. Your physician has access to your medical records, and they also know your current health status. Doctors remain a great resource for optimizing exercises.

Next, gear up for yoga. Head to your favorite retailer and pick up a yoga mat. The variety available on the market has grown in the last few years. Its standard size measures 24 inches wide. Then, pick a length that ranges between 68 inches to 72 - it's up to you. The mat provides cushioning under your feet since it's a barefoot practice. The mat also provides traction for your feet. If you fall in love with yoga and decide to practice the hot version, you'll understand why traction is necessary. The profuse sweat can cause your feet to become slippery.

Weak and/or sore muscles is another reason why you need traction. When you move into Warrior Pose, you'll rely on your thigh and calf muscles to sustain your weight and protect your ankles. As your balance improves, you'll find that it's easier to achieve traction.

For yoga, avoid wearing loose-fitting clothing. When you bend into the Half Moon pose or downward dog, the clothes will fall over your head, or you might feel tangled in them. Instead, look for form-fitting clothing. No shortage of yoga attire exists. Find clothing that doesn't constrict your movements, such as yoga shorts and a tank top or tee. On the shelves, you'll also find yoga socks - nice for chilly days or for those who need additional help achieving traction. If you're worried about slipping, pick up a pair. However, yogis don't wear socks. They strengthen their bodies and hold the poses barefoot.

Once you have purchased your yoga mat and attire, you're ready to start your practice. Some people attend classes. Others use DVDs or digital online classes, practicing at home. Since you picked up this book, keep reading. We've outlined the top poses for seniors seeking to improve their balance. It's that easy!

To start the practice, prepare to engage your mind, spirit, and body as you execute each pose.

Do you need equipment?

Yoga and yoga mats go hand in hand. In a pinch, you can use a large towel. However, a mat won't slip from under you. If you must use a towel, test it for slippage before starting your practice.

You might have heard of yoga equipment, such as blocks and straps. In the 1970s, **B. K. S. Iyengar** introduced the use of yoga props – blocks and straps. Given the long history of the practice, the use of props is still fairly new; therefore, they are not 100% necessary. The theory behind the props is that they bring the floor closer to the participant. In some cases, straps allow participants to execute a full stretch even though they can't clasp their hands together behind their backs. In that case, it's an advantage to have straps at your disposal. If you opt to pick up yoga equipment, avoid using them as crutches. Instead, they should help you ease your way toward not needing them anymore.

Before purchasing equipment, give yoga a few tries. Assess how you feel when you move into Seated Spinal Twist, Cow, and Butterfly poses. If some poses create discomfort or you cannot fully absorb their benefits, then you can pick up yoga props. Use them as aids and work toward moving your body toward the floor without them.

How yoga improves mental health

Yoga emphasizes the connection between the mind and body. Therefore, it helps create clarity, mindfulness, and calmness. By extension, yoga helps reduce stress, anxiety, and cognitive decline. Therefore, the practice helps improve mental health. Some people lean on yoga for stretching, while others turn to it for its mental healing abilities. That's why yoga is a component of well-rounded exercise regimens that help seniors improve their balance.

Over time, individuals have developed yoga practices to address an array of ailments and conditions. For example, if you have trouble sleeping, a yoga practice exists to address it. If you feel discomfort in your back, joints, or wrists, you can easily find yoga practices that address them. (Yoga routines that seek to quiet the mind exist, too!)

Some yoga routines keep students off the areas that experience too much discomfort. Others help students delve into them deeper. For example, the Pigeon pose targets the hips and lower back. It's a challenging position that takes time to fully execute. Nonetheless, instructors will offer variations of the pose so that students do not give up. Then, instructors will ask students to hold the pose for 30 seconds to one minute. The pigeon pose slowly opens the hip flexors and also helps students achieve better digestion. Some students might shy away from this pose, but delving into it provides worthwhile benefits. Giving into pigeon pose helps students and seniors achieve mind over matters. Once you slide out of it, you'll feel stronger physically and mentally.

Yoga safely tests your mental strength. There is no risk that you'll accidentally drop weights on yourself. It's possible to remain in yoga poses for one minute with few risks to your person. Thus, it improves it. Yoga can also quiet your mind.

Yoga differs from meditation. For example, meditation does not require physical movements; yoga does. Yoga combines physical movement with meditation. Once you find a routine that you enjoy, practice it daily. With the routine committed to memory, you'll move through the poses without giving them a second thought. Then, you can close your eyes, empty your mind, and meditate deeper. Meditation sharpens your concentration, focus, and joy – and they all improve your mental health.

Once yoga and exercise become part of your daily life, you'll notice that your self-esteem will improve too.

How yoga improves balance

The mental aspect of yoga is as important as the physical one. Yoga has a purpose – to build harmony between the mind and body. Yoga improves balance while challenging it, and it takes the mind and body. Let's use the Tree pose as an example.

The Tree pose is one of the standing, balancing poses. It requires the practitioner to root one foot into the ground. Then, lift the other off it. Eventually, you'll place your foot on the side of the opposite knee slightly, creating a 90-degree angle. Then, you'll hold the pose for 30 seconds to one minute. Tree pose does challenge some individuals; If you can only hold your foot against the opposite ankle for 30 seconds without tipping over, it's a start. Eventually, you'll have the physical strength, balance, and mental ability to lift it higher and hold it longer.

Yoga addresses alignment. If you hold poses with bad alignment, you'll feel the strain. Thus, yoga improves balance by improving alignment and posture. To optimize results, you'll hold poses for at least 30 seconds. Most instructors ask their students to hold each pose for at least one minute. Therefore, yoga improves balance by opening the body, such as the hip flexors, chest, and shoulders. In addition, it strengthens the muscles. Balance comes from healthy muscle mass and strength. Holding Mountain pose for one minute looks easy enough – but you must *remain engaged in the pose*. You tighten your backside, keep your chest in a proud position, and release tension from your shoulders.

If you lose your focus during yoga, you'll tip over during standing poses. Therefore, yoga improves balance by teaching you to stay in the moment. The alertness, focus, and concentration carry over into daily life. Consistent practice helps you spot risks and make decisions more quickly. If you do trip while walking, you're less likely to fall.

Thus, yoga helps improve balance by strengthening your muscles, improving your mental health, and helping your self-esteem.

Now that you have some background in the practice of yoga, we outline 11 yoga poses that benefit seniors who want to improve their balance.

Yoga Poses for Seniors

We start your yoga practice with standing poses. Then, we'll take you to the floor. For the standing poses, your starting position is feet together. Stand up straight with a slight bend in the knees to avoid locking them. Place your arms at your sides with fingers pointing down without any tension in them. Ensure that there is space between your shoulders and ears by releasing any tension in the neck area. Take a deep breath in and exhale.

Let's get started.

Downward-Facing Dog

The ultimate yoga pose is the downward-facing dog. It provides several health benefits, and it's a staple pose.

Start with both feet planted on the ground and arms and hands at each side.

Release any tension in your shoulders and neck area.

Bend your upper body as if you're attempting to touch your toes.

Once you hinge at the hips as far as you can, start walking your hands forward.

Your goal is to stretch out into a plank position.

Once you reach it, do not reposition your body.

Instead, push off your hands so that you hinge at the hips again.

Attempt to place your feet flat on the ground and stretch your arms.

Your head will go in between your arms as you attempt to touch your elbows to your ears.

Look at your feet through your legs and try to reach your armpits toward your shins.

Hold this position for 30 seconds. Take a deep breath through your nose and exhale it through your nostrils.

To exit Downward-facing Dog, walk your hands back toward your feet. When you almost or successfully touch your toes, raise your torso straight up.

Mountain Pose

From the starting position, create some space between your feet – two to three inches will suffice.

Lift your toes so that you can spread them out.

Then, ground them back onto the floor.

Spread your weight evenly on your feet – avoid leaning on your heels or your toes.

Create energy from your feet and let it rise to your core.

Keep your arms and shoulders relaxed.

Next, relax your head. Hold the pose for 30 seconds.

Inhale deeply through your nose and exhale through your nostrils.

To exit the pose, bring your feet back together and relax your limbs.

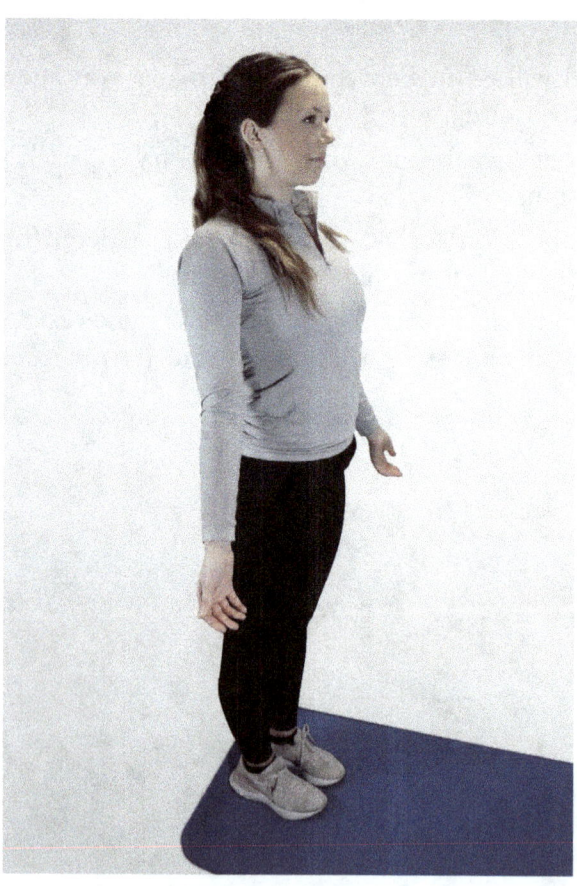

Tree Pose

Now that you know the Mountain pose, you can flow from Mountain pose to the Tree pose.

From a solid Mountain pose, bring your hands together at your chest in a prayer position.

Create tension with your arms – you'll need them to help you balance.

Then, bend your right knee and lift your right foot off the ground.

Touch your left leg with your right foot.

Start by placing your right foot above your left ankle.

Hold the position for 10 seconds.

If you do not tip over, lift your right foot higher and touch your left calf. Hold the position for 10 seconds.

Your goal is to touch your left knee with your right foot and hold the position for 30 seconds without tipping over.

If you start to lean in one direction or another, use your thigh, calf, and ankle to recenter yourself. If the leaning persists, use your arms to recenter yourself.

Lastly, use your mental strength to will yourself back to a centered, balanced position.

After 30 seconds of holding your position, place your right foot back on the ground. Return to Mountain pose and prepare to lift your left foot off the ground.

Bend your left knee and lift your left foot off the ground.

Touch your right leg with your left foot above the ankle and hold the position for 10 seconds.

If you do not tip over, raise your left foot higher.

Touch your right calf with your left foot and hold the position for 10 seconds.

If you do not tip over, raise your left higher and touch your right knee with it.

Hold the position for 30 seconds.

Remember to breathe.

Take in deep breaths every time you lift your foot and release them after placing it on the opposite leg.

If you feel like you might tip over, take in a deep breath and slowly release it.

After 30 seconds, place your left foot back on the ground. Return to Mountain pose and release it.

Warrior II

The Warrior pose has five positions in yoga. We'll focus on Warrior II and Reverse Warrior.

From the starting position, take a breath and lunge your right leg forward.

Exhale and check your posture.

Now, move your left foot so that it's parallel with the back of the yoga mat.

Point your right foot forward.

Turn your torso to face the left side of the room.

Look forward.

Bring your arms to shoulder length, pointing the right hand to the front of the room and the left one to the back.

Sink into the lunge more.

Hold the position for 30 seconds, remembering to continue breathing and exhaling.

Take one last inhale and bring your right leg back to the starting position on the exhale.

Release your arms to your sides.

Now, take a breath and lunge forward with your left leg.

Exhale and check your posture.

Move your right foot so that it's parallel with the back of the yoga mat.

Point your left foot forward.

Turn your torso and face the right side of the room. Look forward.

Bring your arms to shoulder length, pointing the left hand to the front of the room and the left one to the back.

Sink into the lunge more.

Hold the position for 30 seconds, remembering to continue breathing and exhaling.

Take one last inhale and bring your left leg back to the starting position on the exhale.

Release your arms to your sides.

Reverse Warrior

From the starting position, take a breath and lunge your right leg forward.

Exhale and check your posture.

Move your left foot so that it's parallel to the back of the yoga mat. Point your right foot forward.

Bring your arms to shoulder level and face your torso to the front of the room.

Point your right hand forward and your left hand to the back of the room.

Now, arch your back and place your left hand on the back of your right thing.

Bring your right arm over your head and hang your right hand above your head.

Look up at the ceiling.

Hold the position for 30 seconds.

Take a breath and release your right arm and back. In the same motion, flow back to the starting position.

Next, take a breath and lunge your left leg forward.

Exhale and check your posture.

Move your right foot so that it's parallel to the back of the yoga mat. Point your left foot forward.

Bring your arms to shoulder level and face your torso to the front of the room.

Point your left hand forward and your right hand to the back of the room.

Now, arch your back and place your right hand on the back of your right thigh.

Bring your left arm over your head and hang your left hand above your head.

Look up at the ceiling. Hold your position for 30 seconds.

Take a breath and release your left arm and back. In the same motion, flow back to the starting position.

When you become comfortable with Warrior II and Reverse Warrior, flow from one to the other instead of resetting.

Now, let's move to the floor.

The floor yoga poses don't test your balance. Instead, they release your back, hip flexors, and legs. Use Spinal Twist, Butterfly Pose, and Corpse Pose at the end of your yoga practice to cool down. Most instructors use the Cow and Cat poses to warm up their students.

Then, they incorporate Sphinx and Cobra poses within the practice.

Seated Spinal Twist

Sit on your yoga mat and cross your legs.

Take a breath and stretch your arms overhead, forming a V.

Now, bring them back down to touch the floor.

Exhale and touch the floor with your right hand directly in front of you.

Touch the left side with your left hand.

Use your hands to help you twist your back to the left side. Hold the position for 20 seconds and enjoy the stretch.

To enhance the stretch, place your right hand on your left thigh and pull.

Take a breath and exit the stretch by releasing your arms.

Next, take a breath and stretch your arms overhead, forming a V.

Bring them back down to touch the floor.

Exhale and touch the floor with your left hand directly in front of you.

Touch the right side with your right hand.

Use your hands to help you twist your back to the right side.

Hold the position for 20 seconds and enjoy the stretch.

If you watch to stretch further, place your left hand on your right thigh and pull.

Take a breath and exit the stretch by releasing your arms.

Cow Pose

Position yourself on all fours on your yoga mat.

Form a tabletop with your back.

Check your posture by ensuring that you have lined up your shoulders over your wrists and your hips over your knees.

Then, straighten your back.

Now, take a breath and arch your back toward the ceiling.

Fold your head into the arch, bring your belly button to your spine, and tuck in your backside.

Hold the position for 15 seconds. Keep breathing and exhaling. Exhale one more time and release the stretch.

Cat Pose

Position yourself on all fours on your yoga mat.

Form a tabletop with your back.

Check your posture by ensuring that you have lined up your shoulders over your wrists and your hips over your knees.

Then, straighten your back.

Now, take a breath and arch your back to the floor. Look up at the ceiling and try to touch the back of your head with your backside.

Hold the position for 15 seconds and enjoy the stretch.

Keep breathing and exhaling. Exhale one more time and release the stretch.

When you master the cat and cow poses, you can flow from one to the other for a total of 4 times each.

Butterfly Pose

Sit on your yoga mat with your legs crossed.

Now, move your feet so that they touch each other.

Keep your legs open.

Clasp your hands over your feet and place your elbows on your inner thighs.

Push down your things and bring your feet close to your body.

Feel the stretch and hold the position for 30 seconds.

Keep breathing and exhaling.

Exit the position by returning to a cross-legged position or stretch your legs in front of you.

Corpse Pose

For corpse pose, lie down on your back on your yoga mat.

Close your eyes and allow your limbs to relax.

Hold this position for one minute and allow your breath to slow down naturally.

It's a great way to relax at the end of a yoga practice.

Sphinx Pose

Lie down on your stomach on your yoga mat.

Keep your legs close together and your arms at your side.

Now, take a breath and bend your elbows at your sides.

Place your forearms on the mat and exhale.

Push your chest off the mat.

Only lift your chest as far up as your forearms will allow.

They must remain on the mat.

Hold the position for 20 seconds. Keep breathing and exhaling.

Take one more breath and lower your chest back to the mat on the exhale.

Cobra Pose

Lie down on your stomach on your yoga mat.

Keep your legs close together and your arms at your side.

Now, take a breath and place your hands firmly on the mat, palms down.

Push your chest off the mat and straighten your arms.

Avoid overarching your back.

You only need to stretch as much as your arms will allow.

Hold the position for 20 seconds.

Keep breathing and exhaling.

Take one more breath and release the position on the exhale to return to the starting position.

    Now we take a look at advanced balance exercises that you can try on your journey to improving your balance.

Chapter 8 Advanced Balance Exercises

Solid balance, strength, and mental well-being require daily maintenance. You can take a day off here and there, but you must continue replenishing the well. In your journey, it doesn't hurt to explore different resources to keep things fresh. For example, you might have the ability to handle advanced balance exercises. However, you picked up this book to obtain new ideas. Those who start off as beginners also benefit from this chapter; it gives you something to work toward.

We outlined seated, weighted exercises in Chapter 4. Now, we will kick them up a notch. Instead of sitting, perform them standing up. Chapter 8 focuses on exercises that will challenge seniors with advanced flexibility, strength, and balance. It also gives beginners goals to strive toward.

Seniors benefit from weighted exercises, just like professional athletes and young adults. Before completing weight training exercises, consult with your primary care physician. Your physician might recommend that you complete foundational weight training exercises with light weights. In addition, you can perform these exercises with alternatives, such as bottles of water and canned foods. If you receive the green light to weight train, your goal is to add resistance to basic exercises. Some walkers will add 1-pound weights to each hand. The combination of added resistance, walking, and arm movement helps individuals raise their heart rate, burn extra calories, and strengthen their bodies.

Before starting these exercises, test the amount of weight you will use. You want to challenge yourself without causing unnecessary strain or waking up overly sore the next day.

This chapter takes into account that some seniors want to refresh their exercise regimens. You're searching for new ideas. Therefore, we will offer them to you. For beginners, train with the other chapters until you can safely handle the following challenging moves.

Strength training and improved balance

Whether you use canned fruit or 1-lb weights for resistance, strength training is part of a well-rounded exercise routine for seniors trying to improve and maintain their balance.

Standing Weight Exercises

Each of the following moves is standing. The starting position for each is feet hip-width apart with knees slightly bent. Arms hang at your sides with weights, cans of fruit, or water bottles in each hand. Release any tension from your neck and shoulders. Create enough tension in your legs, torso, and back to hold yourself upright. Proper posture ensures that you don't strain any part of your person.

Arm Curl

From the starting position, turn your palms to face the front of the room.

Now, take a breath and release it.

On the release, curl your right arm by bending at the elbow.

Bring the weight to meet your right shoulder without touching it.

Take a breath.

Exhale and release your right arm back to the starting position.

Repeat the sequence a total of eight times on the right side.

Now, switch to the left arm.

From the starting position, turn your palms to face the front of the room.

Now, take a breath and release it.

On the release, curl your left arm by bending at the elbow.

Bring the weight to meet your left shoulder without touching it.

Take a breath.

Exhale and release your left arm back to the starting position.

Repeat the sequence a total of eight times on the left side.

Make it more challenging by curling both arms simultaneously for a total of eight times.

Another option is to alternate arms:

From the starting position, turn your palms to face the front of the room.

Now, take a breath and release it.

On the release, curl your right arm.

Bring the weight to meet your right shoulder without touching it.

Take a breath and release it.

On the release, curl your left arm to meet your left shoulder without touching it.

Simultaneously, release your right arm.

Then, take another breath and exhale.

On the exhale, curl your right arm to meet your right shoulder without touching it. Simultaneously, release your left arm.

Continue the process until you complete 8 curls on the right and left arms.

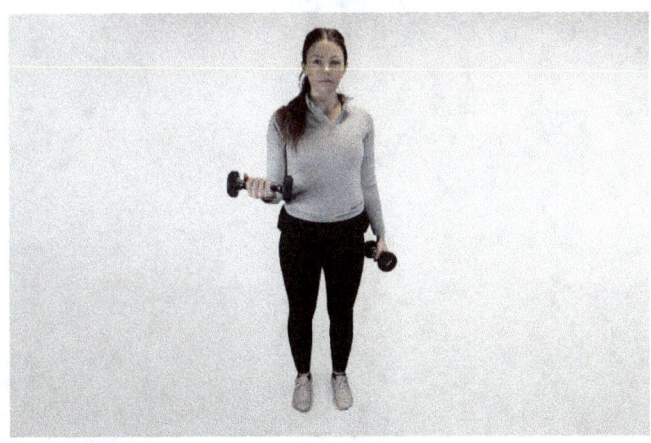

Dumbbell Deadlift

From the starting position, double-check that you are securely holding the weights in each hand.

Bring your hands together so that the weights touch slightly at the sides. Now, take a breath and release it.

On the release, hinge forward from the waist.

Lower your hands as if you will touch your toes.

As you reach down, keep your weights near your legs as if you're about to touch them.

Keep a slight bend in your knees.

Keep your back straight. Squeeze your backside.

Hold the bent position for three seconds.

Take a breath and release it.

On the release, return to the starting position in one swift motion.

Repeat the move a total of eight times.

Dumbbell triceps Extension

From the starting position, place the weight in your left hand.

Check your posture.

Keep a slight bend in both knees.

Now, take a breath. On the exhale, extend your left arm to the ceiling.

Keep it straight.

Keep your back straight.

Next, take another breath. On the exhale, bend your left elbow and lower the weight behind your head.

For support, stretch your right arm toward the ceiling.

Then, bend your right elbow so that your right hand falls over your head in front of your left arm and elbow.

Touch your left elbow with your right hand.

Now, take a breath. On the exhale, raise the weight back up toward the ceiling.

Complete a total of 8 repetitions.

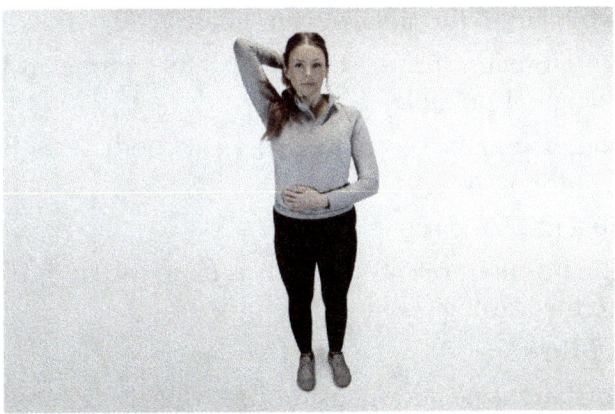

To exit the dumbbell trice extension, release both arms and return to the starting position.

Let's move to the left side.

Switch your weight from your left hand to the right.

Keep a slight bend in both knees.

Now, take a breath. On the exhale, extend your right arm to the ceiling.

Keep it straight.

Keep your back straight.

Next, take another breath. On the exhale, bend your right elbow and lower the weight behind your head.

For support, stretch your left arm toward the ceiling.

Then, bend your left elbow so that your left hand falls over your head in front of your right arm and elbow.

Touch your right elbow with your left hand.

Now, take a breath. On the exhale, raise the weight back up toward the ceiling.

Complete a total of 8 repetitions.

To exit the dumbbell triceps extension, release both arms and return to the starting position.

Another option is to work both triceps simultaneously:

Place a weight in each hand.

From the starting position, bend both knees, slightly hinge forward from the waist, and keep your back straight.

Bring each hand to the sides of your chest.

Now, take a breath. On the exhale, extend both arms behind you at shoulder height if possible.

Take another breath. On the exhale, curl both arms back toward the sides of your chest.

Complete a total of 8 repetitions.

To exit the position, release your arms from the sides of your chest and return to the starting position.

Dumbbell Row

From the starting position, ensure that you have a weight in each hand.

Slightly bend your knees and hinge forward from the waist.

Keep your back straight.

Let your arms hang in front of you.

Align them with your shoulders.

Now, take a breath and release it.

On the release, lift both arms toward your chest by bending your elbows.

Keep your elbows next to your body.

Take another breath and exhale.

On the exhale, release both arms.

Repeat the sequence eight times.

Overhead Press

From the starting position, ensure that you have a weight in each hand.

Slightly bend your knees. Now, take a breath and release it.

On the release, lift both arms above your head.

On the lift, keep your arms near your head.

When you reach the top, your arms should lightly touch your ears. Plus, the weights should slightly touch at the top.

To exit the position, take a breath and exhale it.

On the exhale, release your arms back to the starting position.

Repeat the exercise eight times.

Front Raise

From the starting position, ensure that you have a weight in each hand.

Slightly bend your knees.

Keep your back straight.

Bring your hands together so that weights lightly touch.

Now, take a breath and release it.

On the release, raise both arms as high as you can without going above shoulder height.

Once you reach a comfortable height, take a breath and exhale it. On the exhale, lower both arms to the starting position.

Repeat the exercise eight times.

If both arms are too challenging, alternate them.

From the starting position, ensure that you have a weight in each hand.

Slightly bend your knees.

Keep your back straight.

Bring your hands together so that the weights lightly touch. Now, take a breath and release it. On the release, raise your right as high as you can without going above shoulder height.

Take a breath and exhale.

On the exhale, lower your right arm to the starting position and raise your left arm without going above shoulder height.

Repeat the sequence eight times.

Another option is to focus on one arm at a time. Raise your right arm eight times. Then, raise your left arm eight times.

Dumbbell Squat

Let's turn the dumbbell squat into a compound exercise, which is among the best for strengthening the body and improving balance.

From the starting position, ensure that you have a weight in each hand.

Slightly bend your knees.

Keep your back straight.

Release any tension from your neck and shoulder area.

Bring your hands together so that the weights lightly touch at the sides.

Now, take a breath and release it.

On the release, bend the knees and move into a squat position.

Squeeze your backside.

Don't let your knees pass your toes.

Avoid arching your back or leaning forward.

Hold the squat for three seconds.

Then, take a breath and exhale it.

On the exhale, return to the starting position.

Repeat the move a total of eight times.

Now, let's make it more challenging:

From the starting position, prepare yourself to squat.

From the squat position, you will exit it and lift your arms up over your head in one swift motion. Take a breath and release it.

On the release, lift your body up and your arms over your head.

Next, take another breath and exhale it.

On the exhale, lower your arms and bend your knees so that you move into a squat position in one swift motion.

Repeat the sequence a total of eight times.

You can also perform the above exercise with a light resistance band. If you don't have one, pick one up from your favorite retailer. Resistance bands come in handy for team exercises. So do lightweight medicine balls and balance balls. Let's explore some team exercises in Chapter 9.

Chapter 9 It Takes Two: Team Exercises

Friendships and relationships become more important in later years. Although the statistics show that seniors don't experience more depression than their younger counterparts, seniors are at risk for other mental health issues. For example, you might feel isolated or lonely.

One way to stave off feelings of loneliness and isolation and to maintain good balance is to enlist a friend or more who will exercise with you.

Some communities are great for providing group classes at local senior centers and recreation centers. When there is no group class available (or you can't make it), invite a friend over to your home or head over to theirs. You can also head to a local park and enjoy the sun with your team exercise session.

Benefits of finding an exercise partner

Life is a series of cycles, and the cycles contribute to the loneliness and isolation that seniors might experience in their later years. Ideally, your children will move out of your home and start their own lives. However, when they do, they have less time to visit. Then, your spouse might pass away before you do, or friends may pass.

The benefits of finding an exercise partner are manyfold. Mainly, you each have someone that supports the other person. You can encourage and cheer for each other. After your workout sessions, you can also share some laughs, meals, and conversations.

Challenge each other and support each other

It's very easy to become complacent and go through the motions of exercise. If you can lift your arms over your head, you might feel like that's good enough. However, the muscles need tension too. Your goal is to keep improving and avoiding plateauing. Therefore, an exercise partner challenges you.

Share Ideas

One person can come up with ideas. With two people, you can bounce them off each other. These ideas don't have to focus on exercise. Maybe you're searching for new recipes, or you're thinking of changing your insurance provider. Thanks to your improved brain power and mental capacity, you can have these conversations with your exercise buddy. They can make suggestions or say something that will spark a solution.

Social Connection

Humans remain social creatures, and they need interaction with others. Many seniors join groups and clubs so that they can have that social connection. Others move to retirement communities so that social connection is always available to them. Another option is visiting your community's senior center. The best ones provide meals, interaction with others, and several activities to participate in.

Partner exercise makes it more fun

Whether or not exercise is fun depends on who you ask. For professional athletes, exercise is work. They probably enjoy it since exercise improves their performance and income-earning potential. Some amateurs take exercise seriously because it's their path toward winning events or paving their way to the Olympics.

Some average people take exercising seriously too. They have a goal in mind, and they want to achieve it. For example, before summer rolls around, they want to look great in a bathing suit. Those who live in sunny areas know that bathing suit season is year-round. Thus, there is no time off.

Once you reach your Golden Years, you can still have vanity goals. After years of raising families, working, and being members of their community, most seniors simply want to enjoy the rest of their lives, and exercise is an enjoyable activity. Even if you want to improve your balance, you can enjoy the process.

Team exercises help motivate partners. That's why partner exercise makes it more fun!

Let's look at some exercises that you can enjoy with a buddy.

You can perform all of these exercises without any equipment. To add to the intensity, we recommend obtaining a lightweight medicine ball or a large stability ball. A resistance band will also make some of the exercises more challenging and fun.

The starting position for each exercise will be standing side by side with your exercise buddy. Stand with feet hip-width apart and a slight bend in the knees. Let your arms and hands hang at your sides.

Medicine Ball Toss

From the starting position, each person takes three steps away from the other.

Then, turn and face one another.

Judge the distance. If this provides enough space to toss a ball to each other, stay there.

One partner will grab the ball and begin tossing.

Start by tossing the ball underhanded.

From a standing position, hold the ball in front of you.

Now, hinge at the hips and lean slightly forward so that you can bring the ball in between your legs.

Place your hands under the ball and create tension in your triceps.

Take a breath and release it.

On the release, toss the ball to your partner.

The first few tries should help you test your strength and obtain a feel for the ball and toss. However, your goal is to toss it so that your partner doesn't move too far to their left or right to catch it.

If your toss falls short distance-wise, determine if both of you need to come closer together.

Each partner will toss the ball eight times.

If you like, you can perform this exercise sitting down too.

Medicine Ball Pass

From the starting position, each partner turns away from the other so that they stand back-to-back.

Each partner stands up straight.

Avoid leaning on each other.

However, you should feel each other's backs.

One partner will pick up the medicine ball and hold it in front of their partner.

The partner with the ball takes a breath and exhales it.

On the exhale, they will turn to their right and wait for their partner to receive the ball.

When your exercise buddy takes a breath, take one too.

Then, release it.

On the release, turn to your left, ready to receive the ball.

Next, the partner with the ball will secure it in their arms.

Take a breath and release it.

On the release, they will turn to their right, ready to pass on the ball.

The partner without the ball will also take a breath and release it.

On the release, they will turn to their left, ready to receive the ball.

Each partner will pass the ball and receive it eight times.

Next, stay standing back-to-back, but the partners will switch the side previously used to receive and pass the ball.

The partner that held the ball first should hold it first again. This time, they will turn to the left and pass the ball.

Take a breath and exhale.

On the exhale, turn to your left, ready to pass the ball.

The partner will take a breath and exhale in sync with the other.

On the exhale, turn to your right, ready to receive the ball.

The partner with the ball will secure it in their arms.

Take a breath and exhale it.

On the exhale, turn to your left, ready to pass the ball.

Your partner will breathe and exhale with you.

On the exhale, turn to your right, ready to receive the ball.

Each partner will pass the ball and receive it eight times.

Back-to-Back Squat

From the starting position, each partner will turn away from the other so that you end up back-to-back.

Stand up straight and check your posture.

Keep your feet hip-width apart with a slight bend in the knees.

In this exercise, you will lean on each other.

However, do not use each other as a crutch. Each partner should carry their weight.

Before the first squat, check that each of you is in the position.

For support, place your hands on your hips, thighs, or cross them on your chest.

Next, take a breath and exhale it. On the exhale, both partners will squat down.

Create tension in your body without tipping over your partner. Hold the squat for three seconds.

Then, take a breath and exhale it. On the exhale, both partners will stand up again.

Squat eight times.

Lateral Squat Walk

This exercise requires timing, effort, and trust from both exercise buddies.

From the starting position, each partner will turn away from the other.

Situate yourselves back-to-back.

Each partner will check their posture.

You should feel each other's back.

However, avoid leaning on each other.

If you both stand up straight, you'll feel each other's backs but don't lean too much.

Both partners will take a breath and exhale.

On the exhale, both partners will squat and hold the position for three seconds.

Then, one partner will step out laterally to the right while the other steps out laterally to the left. Once you both take the step, squat again.

Return to the starting position by pushing off the right foot for one partner and the left foot for the other.

Repeat the lateral squat sequence eight times.

Now, the partners will switch the foot that they used.

From the starting position, each partner will remain turned away from the other and back-to-back.

Check your posture and feel each other's backs. Avoid over-leaning on each other.

Move into a squat position and hold it for three seconds.

Take a breath and exhale it.

On the exhale, the first partner will step laterally to their left, and the other will step laterally to their right.

Then, each partner will squat.

Hold the squat for three seconds.

Take a breath and exhale it; on the exhale, step back to the original squat position.

Repeat the lateral squat on this side eight times.

Seesaw Resistance Band

Resistance bands are great for partner exercises. If you do not have one, that's OK. You can use a towel instead.

From the starting position, step away from your partner enough to stretch out the resistance band. Then, face each other.

Holding the edge of the resistance band, each partner will take a breath and exhale it.

The first partner will reach their arms up in the air.

The second partner will squat. Both partners will take a breath and release it.

On the release, the first partner will move into a squat in one swift motion.

The second partner will reach their arms up into the air.

Each partner will complete 8 reaches to their air and 8 squats.

Seesaw Resistance Band with a Twist

From the starting position, each partner will hold one end of a resistance band or towel.

Step laterally away from each other until you stretch your resistance band.

Each partner will face the front of the room.

The partner on the right side of the room will begin the exercise.

Twist your torso to the right of the room, pulling on the resistance band with both hands.

Keep both feet planted on the floor and hold the position for three seconds.

The second partner will remain facing the front of the room and hold the resistance band.

After three seconds, the first partner will release the twist, and the second partner will twist to the left side of the room. Hold the position for three seconds.

The second partner will face the front of the room, holding the resistance band.

Each partner will complete 8 twists.

Then, the partners will switch sides. The first partner will twist to the left eight times.

The second partner will twist to the right eight times.

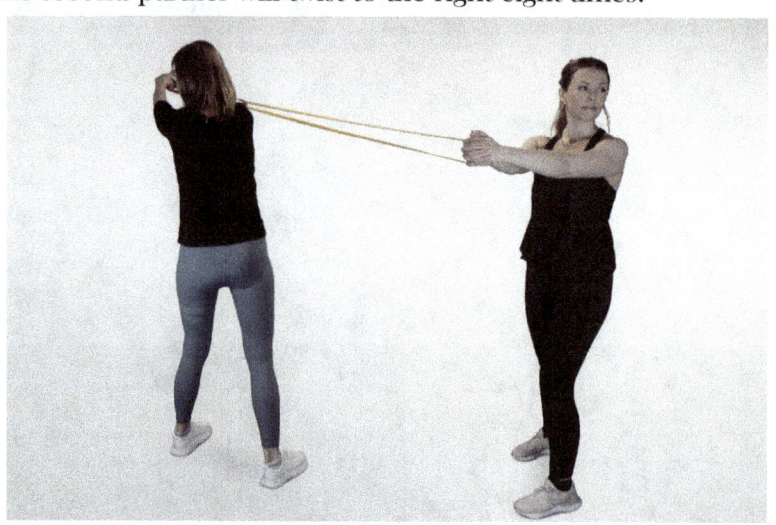

Resistance Band triceps Kickbacks

This exercise does require a resistance band.

From the starting position, one partner will hold the middle of the resistance band.

Then, the partner will hold both ends of it. Both partners will walk away from each other until they sufficiently stretch the band.

Face each other and grip your share of the band.

The partner holding the ends of the resistance band will enter the row position.

From the standing position, slightly bend the knees.

Then, hinge forward from the waist. Next, pull the resistance band toward the back of the room as you extend your arms backward in one swift motion.

Pull the resistance band to work your triceps eight times.

Now, switch with your partner.

Stretches

Stretching with a partner is also fun. Let's take a look at some partner stretches.

Sitting V Stretch

For this partner stretch, both individuals will sit on the ground. To make it comfortable, use a yoga mat. Plus, we will offer two variations.

Both partners will face each other. Each will open their legs and make a V-shape.

Then, both partners will touch each other's feet with their feet.

Depending on how this feels, make adjustments.

For a wider stretch, make the V wider. If you're not ready for a wide stretch, make the V narrower.

Once both partners feel comfortable, reach for each other's arms.

Facing each other straight on, hold onto each other's forearms.

Both partners will take a breath.

The first partner will exhale and lean forward as the second one exhales and leans back.

The first partner will go deeper into the stretch when the second one leans back.

Hold the position for 10 seconds.

It's up to each partner to let the other one know if they can go deeper into the stretch or not. Then, the second partner must listen for those verbal cues.

After 10 seconds, both partners will take a breath and exhale.

On the exhale, both partners will return to their sitting, upright position.

Breathe again.

On the exhale, the second partner will lean forward as the first one leans back. Hold this position for 10 seconds.

For the second variation, each partner will hold the other one's hand.

To make it easy, as you're facing each other, both partners will reach toward the other with their right hand.

Now, clasp it.

Take a breath and exhale it.

On the exhale, both partners will lean their left arms' over their heads and stretch to the right side of the room. Hold the stretch for 10 seconds.

After 10 seconds, take a breath and exhale it.

On the exhale, return to the sitting, upright position.

Now, switch hands by reaching toward each other with your left hand.

Clasp them. Take a breath and exhale it.

On the exhale, stretch your right arm over your head and lean toward the left side of the room.

Hold the position for 10 seconds.

After 10 seconds, take a breath and exhale.

On the exhale, return to the upright, sitting position.

Exit the stretch by folding your legs into yourself.

For example, you can sit cross-legged. Then, stand up.

You've made it to the end of our list of exercises and stretches for seniors who want to improve their balance. Congratulations!

Hopefully, you have tried all of these exercises and stretches so that you can gauge where you stand physically and, more importantly, how well you can balance.

Our final chapter focuses on what you can do if you experience a setback. Let's dive in.

Chapter 10 Dealing with Setbacks

We outlined several opportunities to test your current physical abilities and limitations throughout the previous chapters. We also inserted tips and reminders to help you prevent injuries, such as over-straining the muscles. Setbacks can occur outside of your control. For example, you may have an old injury that could flare up again. When such setbacks occur, it's vital to figure out a way around them. Even minor setbacks can cause you to lose your motivation or ability to continue improving your balance. Although these setbacks can occur without warning, it's essential to take steps to prevent them, such as scheduling your annual checkup with your physician.

Then, there are the setbacks that occur from a lack of focus, stretching, or motivation. We discussed the importance of training with a positive mindset. It will help you focus and improve your mental health. Moreover, you are less likely to injure yourself by accident.

Positive attitude toward having setbacks

Very few people find joy in experiencing an injury during exercise. An exercise injury impacts more than your training sessions; it also affects your ability to complete daily tasks. Even though you cannot exercise for a few days, maintain a positive attitude.

All setbacks aren't physical – some are mental. The body doesn't perform the same daily. Some days it's more flexible than others. Some days you'll feel stronger than others too. In addition, some people set weight or fitness goals and have trouble reaching them. They consider their failure to meet their goals a setback.

The good news is that in most cases, you can overcome your setbacks. We'll explore how in Chapter 10.

Some common injuries seniors experience during exercise include:

- Sprains
- Strains
- Muscle pulls
- Joint stress
- Shin splints

Sprains impact the ligaments, while stretching impacts the tendons. In both cases, the injuries only lead to stiffness or soreness. However, coupled with older age, they might feel more harmful and worrisome. In severe cases, the injuries will take you off your feet longer.

Mild sprains and strains take two weeks to heal on average. To avoid making the injury worse, avoid strenuous exercise for eight weeks. Instead of performing standing and weight exercises, work on floor exercises, stretches, and yoga.

Mild muscle pulls take between three to six weeks to heal. After pulling a muscle, avoid exercising altogether. After a few days, try stretching and assess how you feel. Then, engage in physical activity that does not involve the injured area.

Anyone who has experienced shin splints will tell you that they are not pleasant. Repetitive activity and strenuous standing exercises often lead to shin splints. If you go for a lengthy walk, you might feel the effects the next day. Severe shin splints can take months to heal. Mild cases might need a few days of rest.

If you experience joint stress, see your physician. Joint stress is a sign of arthritis. Those with mild cases of joint stress benefit from exercise. You might need a specialized exercise regimen if you have a severe case.

This book focuses on exercise that helps you improve your balance. None of these exercises should cause severe discomfort or stress on your joints. They will help you stretch your muscles, lubricate your joints, and strengthen your core without having to do sit-ups.

Importance of rest and rehabilitation if an injury occurs

The medical community believes that seniors should complete 150 minutes of exercise per week. Ideally, you'll divide that chunk of time into daily 30-minute increments.

If you experience a physical setback that requires rest and rehabilitation, go ahead and rest. Resting doesn't mean sitting on the couch all day and watching television. It doesn't mean avoiding standing on your feet all day.

When you need to rehabilitate an injury, examine your exercise alternatives. For example, yoga. Sphinx and cobra poses are great for the arms and back. Neither pose requires you to stand on your feet. Seated spinal twists and butterfly pose are also great for your back, obliques, and core – they don't require you to stand on your feet either.

If you need to rest your legs, you can always perform the seated chair exercises we outlined. Even though your legs might be experiencing fatigue, you can still strengthen your arms. Plus, seated chair exercises are gentle enough for your legs that they can help you rehabilitate muscle pulls, strains, and sprains.

Everyone needs to rest as much as they need to sleep, between seven to nine hours daily. Older muscles, bones, and joints require a little more rest than 30-somethings.

If an injury occurs, take a few steps to reduce the impact.

Rest for at least two days. Rest simply means avoiding long walks, strenuous exercise, and standing for long periods.

Ice and heat the area. Professionals debate whether heat or cold works best to reduce inflammation and soreness. Therefore, consider using both. Place a cold compress on the area that has discomfort for 15 minutes. Then, replace the cold with heat. Leave it on for another 15 minutes. The heat creates a soothing sensation, while the cold causes the blood to rush to the injured area. Many people believe that blood has healing properties. Therefore, your own body can heal itself with the right strategies.

In a few days, test the area. Do you remember what caused the injury? If a standing exercise caused it, complete floor or seated exercises before returning to standing ones.

Watch your diet. You want to eat foods that nourish your body, not hinder it. Eat good helpings of fruits, vegetables, and protein. Avoid overly processed foods containing high amounts of sugar, oils, and fats.

After a week, try exercising other areas of your body to see how it responds to the physical activity. You might experience some soreness, but it's the kind that indicates that your muscles are becoming stronger.

Importance of continuing your exercise – develop a routine

Consistency is critical for improving and maintaining your balance. Even if you experience a physical setback, do your best to practice alternative exercises. If you go for a pleasant half-hour walk today, you might feel winded toward the end. However, if you keep walking for half an hour daily for a week, you'll notice that you feel less winded at the end – that's consistency kicking in.

If you take a break for a week and start walking again, you'll feel better after the first walk. It's almost like starting over again.

Instead of putting your body through that kind of stress, develop a routine. Use your living situation to your advantage. For example, if you live in a retirement community, gather some of your neighbors and exercise together after breakfast. If you live at home, exercise with your spouse, family members, or alone.

Then, clean up and seize the day. Suppose you have busy mornings because you help watch your grandchildren. In that case, you might save your physical activities for the afternoon or evening. The point is to develop a schedule that works for you, your life, and your commitments.

More importantly, developing a routine will stave off injuries because you keep your muscles stretched and strong.

After experiencing a setback, the worst thing to do is give up. A study found that 73% of individuals who set fitness-related New Year's resolutions don't make it to the end of the year, let alone the first month. Moreover, many stop exercising altogether. *Not exercising* has severe – and lifelong – effects, including a higher risk of heart disease, obesity, and diabetes. Plus, seniors will experience the loss of muscle mass and strength, which deteriorates balance.

Now that you have made it to the end of this book, you can improve your balance today. You may have already tried several of our exercises. If you have not, start with our stretching exercises, and then follow the rest of the chapters. You have already taken the first step toward strengthening your muscles. Next, make it a routine to continually improve your balance. Seniors benefit from physical activity daily – at least 30 minutes.

We know that you can improve your balance and quality of life in these golden years.

Thank you for reading, and happy exercising!

Here's another book by Scott Hamrick that you might like

Free Bonuses from Scott Hamrick

Hi seniors!

My name is Scott Hamrick, and first off, I want to THANK YOU for reading my book.

Now you have a chance to join my exclusive "workout for seniors" email list so you can get the ebook below for free as well as the potential to get more ebooks for seniors for free! Simply click the link below to join.

P.S. Remember that it's 100% free to join the list.

Access your free bonuses here
https://livetolearn.lpages.co/balance-exercises-for-seniors-paperback/